Sweet Distress

how our love affair with feelings has fuelled the current mental health crisis

(and what we can do about it)

Gillian Bridge

Crown House Publishing Limited
www.crownhouse.co.uk

First published by

Crown House Publishing Ltd
Crown Buildings, Bancyfelin, Carmarthen, Wales, SA33 5ND, UK
www.crownhouse.co.uk

and

Crown House Publishing Company LLC
PO Box 2223, Williston, VT 05495, USA
www.crownhousepublishing.com

First published 2020.

Crown House Publishing has no responsibility for the persistence or accuracy of URLs for external
or third-party websites referred to in this publication, and does not guarantee that any content on
such websites is, or will remain, accurate or appropriate.

British Library Cataloguing-in-Publication Data
A catalogue entry for this book is available
from the British Library.

Print ISBN 978-178583467-7
Mobi ISBN 978-178583476-9
ePub ISBN 978-178583477-6
ePDF ISBN 978-178583478-3

LCCN 2019953044

This book is dedicated to
independent thinkers everywhere.

Acknowledgements

My thanks to my editor Emma Tuck, who by using her cool classical thinking to temper my hot-hatch impulses brought it to its present beautifully balanced state.

And thanks to my wonderful, ever patient, supportive and loving family and friends.

Contents

Acknowledgements .... *i*

Introduction **1**

Chapter 1 **Self-pleasuring in every way** **7**
Addicted to self 9

Chapter 2 **A fixation on fixing life?** **13**

Chapter 3 **In which sugar and resilience come together** **19**
What is a man? 21

Chapter 4 **Hot stuff and cool reason** **25**

Chapter 5 **A balancing (of emotions) act** **33**
Parents' takeaway for balancing emotion 40
Educators' takeaway for balancing emotion 43

Chapter 6 **Language matters** **51**
Parents' takeaway for boosting pro-mental health language skills 55
Educators' takeaway for boosting pro-mental health language skills 56

Chapter 7 **Up and down and round and round we go** **59**
Dopamine 60
Oxytocin 61
Other substances 66
Nicotine 67
Cannabis 69
Alcohol 70
Parents' takeaway for protecting youngsters against substance-related problems 71
Educators' takeaway for protecting youngsters against substance-related problems 73

Chapter 8   **The less sweet sweet spot** **77**

   Universities 79

   Happiness 82

   Single interest communities 84

   Beam me up, Scottie! 87

   Parenting Goldilocks (or hitting the sweet spot) 91

   Educating Goldilocks (or hitting the sweet spot) 93

Chapter 9   **'I'dentity** **99**

   Am I really who I think I am? 101

   Parenting to support a strong enough sense of
   identity 108

   Educating to support a strong enough sense of
   identity 112

**Chapter 10 Prehab beats rehab (or how to build
   resilience)** **115**

   Sneaking feelings 125

   Parenting for resilience 128

   Educating for resilience 130

Chapter 11 A call to action **133**

   Exercise 133

   Diet 135

   Substances 136

   External observations, aka criticism 137

Grand finale **139**

   Fitter, healthier brains (and less emotional flab) .. 139

References *143*

Let us not talk ourselves into far greater mental distress, even as we believe ourselves to be talking our way out of it.

A Great Big
Emotional Wankfest?

I do believe (even passionately, if it helps) that the answer to the above question is a great big YES. Yes, we've been living in a gross-out world of personal emotional self-indulgence and sentiment for decades now: decades which, for all the alluring (and, yes, passionate) rhetoric of celebrities, of pressure groups and of parts of the media, have seen the nation's mental health worsening and not improving, as they seem to imply that it *should* be doing, given how much more emotionally articulate we're supposedly becoming. It's a terrible, and often tragic, irony.

We're actually in a crisis of vast proportions. Youngsters are dying needlessly, everyone seems confused and overwhelmed by often contradictory information and, to me, it all seems as insane as it does unnatural. How can a species that is supposed to be as intelligent as ours be self-harming in this way? Quite frankly, it's getting much too late for the niceties; far too many of us have been pussyfooting around personal and cultural sensitivities, even as the nation's mental health has been racing downhill on a Teflon-coated sledge. It's time for some tough talking. Every way we turn there is increasing evidence that families, schools, universities — the whole societal shebang, in fact — is being overwhelmed by an extraordinary epidemic of mental ill health. And that means real lives, real people who are suffering every day and desperately looking for the help that just can't be made available to enough of us, in a short enough space of time, to make it possible for such lives to be lived as fully and robustly as they could and should be lived.

Notice that I say mental *ill* health, because we have become so 'into' the problem that people have started to use the phrase 'mental health' to mean 'negative mental health', and that surely is one of the most worrying developments of all. We no longer seem to have any real concept of *positive* mental health.

What a bizarre, unnatural mess we appear to have landed our-selves in.

I've already talked at much greater length about the problems we're facing (as well as what we can do about them) in my book *The Significance Delusion*,[1] but that goes into a lot of background, a lot of detail and maybe a tad more science than is needed to get the basic message across – although it is essential reading if you really want to understand the hows and whys of our current crises of identity and wellbeing. This time, because we have no time to spare, I'm going to go straight for the functional jugular.

What I want, what you want, what we all want, is a solution to the crisis, and with as little reference to 'deep science' as we can get away with in order to explain cause and effect. I'm planning to pro-vide that in as straightforward a way as possible.

First, I will be focusing primarily on the mental health of young people – of children and adolescents. By looking at what is going on for them I will, inevitably, be looking at the entire family tree, the whole evolution of mental health, which will include everyone else's, too. I will also, inevitably, be looking at where and how we can all play our parts in making a difference and have a role in improving the lives of those around us. Because we all can and should – no, *must* – if we genuinely want things to change. And that is one of the most positive and empowering things that can come out of the cur-rent mental health mess.

And so, by a sort of benign contagion, with viral efficiency, I hope that we can sort out many of the problems fairly swiftly. Pressure groups are constantly demanding huge policy shifts that will effect massive social change. Such things take time and significant resources. Can we wait that long?

It is far easier to make smaller everyday changes that will impact directly on the people we care about, and so spread like a meme – the meme of mental good health.

Let's make that our resolution: to focus on the things that we, that I, can do in small incremental shifts to foster *good mental health* in those we love and in anyone else who comes into our world. By taking on the challenge at a personal level – even when that goes against the grain if we think institutions should be dealing with it – I believe

---

1   Gillian Bridge, *The Significance Delusion: Unlocking Our Thinking for Our Children's Future* (Carmarthen: Crown House Publishing, 2016).

that we can end up feeling more in control of our lives. And that is especially important at a time when it can often feel as if we're being overwhelmed and disempowered by external forces taking over so many of the roles we used to assume for ourselves.

Personal control over mental and physical health, in particular, is something which some of us feel has been pulled out from underneath us by politicians, institutions and even the media, which is endlessly assaulting us with lifestyle 'advice' and campaigns. Campaigns which often appear to set one shiny new inspirational lifestyle movement against another equally exciting, promising and intoxicating one: clean living; detoxifying your self, your environment, your shelves, your social media accounts, your apps; mindfulness; slow living, slow eating, slow TV and radio, living more like a sloth; green exercise, blue exercise, high-intensity interval training, yoga, aerobics, cold water exercise; playdates for the over sixties, sessions combating loneliness for teens ... and on and on it goes. All these brilliant new ideas, initiatives and innovations! It can feel like there is a new one for every new dawn.

How can anyone 'normal' feel competent to decide what's right, what's best (for them) and what's going to work in the long term, let alone feel as if they are entitled to decide for themselves? And if it's hard to know which celebrity-endorsed approach is going to be most effective in getting any of us from couch potato to triathlete before life finally calls time, how much harder is it going to be to sort out the mental health wheat from the maybe just mental chaff? It's all enough to do your head in!

I want to make it easier for all of us. With a personal back catalogue that includes teaching, lecturing, addiction therapy, brain damage therapy, psychotherapy, counselling, autism specialisation and executive coaching, and with time spent working in organisations ranging from schools and universities to prisons and elite private members' clubs to banks and international businesses, I have been able to gather an extraordinary amount of diverse, occasionally strange but often surprisingly relevant material. This includes the common neurobiological features of addiction, autism and criminality, and the importance of storytelling in avoiding post-traumatic stress disorder (PTSD), all of which gives me a slightly different perspective on many behavioural problems. And I have worked with a wonderful and colourful selection of living breathing humans who have generously provided me with that material. What I have been able to discover is that people often have far more in common, in terms of their underlying make-up, their brains and their behaviour, than much academic research (with its inevitably narrower focus) is able to pick up on, which gives me quite a 'head start' when it comes to recognising and understanding the links between our behaviour (whether 'average' or rather less so), our ways of communicating and our brain health.

Drawing on my experience of prisoners, addicts, teenagers, mental health clients of every age, people on the autism spectrum and those with brain damage, as well as my wide knowledge base, I believe that I'm very well equipped to comment on the main presenting problems of the day, as well as in just about the best possible position to consider one of the most important weapons we have in our fight against them. That is *resilience*, the human quality that above all others keeps us strong when things get tough.

I have seen it all, and then quite a bit more, and that has given me an overview of what is working for those individuals who are able to keep it together, and what isn't working for those who sadly can't.

Resilience isn't wellbeing, it isn't self-esteem, it isn't mindfulness, it isn't happiness. It has been around a lot longer than any on-trend, single solution sound bite might suggest, and it's both simpler and more complicated than any of them. Without going into a huge amount of detail at this point, I can say that it's just about as close to being the opposite of self-gratification as you can get.

The Significance Delusion deals with resilience in detail; in this book I will stick mostly to aspects of it that are relevant to some very specific problems – the ones that give us such worrying headlines. Without suggesting any hierarchy of significance, I have put together a list of those problems which seem to be most frequently cited as being sources of mental distress:

- Stress
- Loneliness
- Anxiety
- Depression
- Body image
- Eating disorders
- Social media
- Suicidal thoughts
- Substance and behavioural disorders

- Perfectionism
- Academic pressures
- Bullying
- Fear of missing out (FOMO)

I might have added family structures or the concerns that social commentators and politicians will often point to as being the real underlying problems, such as poverty, or lack of adequate housing, or job insecurity, or, or, or ... But actually I think my list stands (although you may want to add your own concerns to it), and that is because I don't believe that societal issues are *inevitable* triggers of individual reactions. One person's anxiety-provoking situation may be another person's incentive to do something radical and creative in response to it. By keeping my list to those things that are less to do with hard, objectively measurable problems, and more to do with qualitative human experiences, I want to stay in the realm of the personal and stay out of the realm of the pressure group. That way lies true empowerment – of you, of me and of real people everywhere. *We* can make lives better. *They* are absolutely not the only ones with the power to do it.

I will be taking a look at how these matters have come to be the insurmountable emotional problems they are, and I will also be taking a few potshots at some of the things that I think have contributed to turning life events that may, at other times or in other places (perhaps more resilient ones?), have been little more than nuisances or inconveniences into sources of genuine psychic pain. Some of these may seem both surprising and counter-intuitive, but I hope my revelations will eventually make sense and, more importantly, point the way to solutions.

I've given the book, and especially this chapter, titles which I hope may both stimulate some fresh thinking and highlight one of its main themes – that of the self-gratification and self-indulgence of appetites. As it's being written at a time when we're already being asked to reflect on the relative healthfulness of our past lives, it also gels rather sweetly with my take on the relationship between physical and psychological appetites. We're having to accept that sugar – the substance which has tempted and tickled our taste buds for so many years – has been one of the root causes in the downward spiral of our physical health. Now I want us to consider whether our mental health problems may also be down to sweet and attractive substances which have been just as positively marketed and promoted to us, and also involve quite a lot of self-gratification.

We have finally realised that we must change our lifestyles if we want to live longer and better physical lives, so perhaps we should also learn to accept alternative ways of thinking and living if we want to achieve the healthier and happier mental outcomes of which we're so desperately in need. Even if that means giving up some tasty things we've come to love. I believe that it is completely doable. Although we may have lost touch with the concept of good mental health, underneath it all we are just a species of animal, and like other animals most of us still have a healthy survival instinct. We may be teetering on the entrance to the emergency department of life at the moment, but there is help on the way.

Think of this book as a crash-team approach to mental health – fast, hard and life-saving, but not necessarily comfortable or sensitive to feelings. However, it will focus on offering that help in a practical way, so at the end of Chapters 5–10, which deal with specific issues, there will be sections of particular value to parents, would-be parents, teachers and those in the business of young people's mental health, such as counsellors and therapists. For simplicity I will use the headings 'parents' and 'educators', but I hope these 'takeaway' sections will be of use to everyone, because the bottom line is that we all have a part to play in the mental health of those around us, and we should all take the applause when we start to make a positive difference.

Likewise, towards the end of the book I have gathered together some selected material into 'a call to action' which will reiterate and reinforce some of the most practical and achievable lifestyle advice mentioned in the book. The idea is to make it all as memorable and accomplishable as possible. We *can* make that difference!

Chapter 1

Self-pleasuring in every way

As I write, we are living out the consequences of our longstanding sugar habit, and it's not a very nice place to be. It's not just the physical reality that a moment on the lips has led to a lifetime on the hips – leaving many of us obese and at great risk of debilitating illness – but it's also that the pursuit of instant and accessible sweetness has affected our thought processes and priorities. The bottom line, sadly, is that anything which encourages us to live in and for the short term, and do what gives us immediate pleasure, is bound to trip us up in the longer term. Other animals may get away with living like that, but they don't have to run nuclear plants, manage traffic flow on motorways or take A levels. We have to look after our species' long-term interests, too.

The trouble is that once you're hooked on short-termism, it's really hard to give it up and it becomes a tyranny. Just think about soap operas. Once upon a time a programme like *Coronation Street* could spend weeks on a spat between two middle-aged women who disapproved of one another's dress sense. But now the producers seem to be terrified that if there isn't a murder or a rape in nearly every episode the programme won't grab viewers' attention, or apparently reflect 'real life' (a question of chicken and egg there, I think). And see, I'm now using the word 'terrified' when I originally wrote 'fearful', because I'm terrified that without going to extremes of emotion you won't want to read my book. It's a verbal sugar rush.

We seem to have no time to take time, which is nonsense, of course, especially in the westernised world. Most of us have never had so much time free from basic drudgery, or fighting, or farming. But we want everything *right now*, and we want it all to be simple and sweet; no unnecessary chewing, no exhausting effort. And therein lies one of the main problems at the heart of the current mental health crisis – we have been lulled into thinking that everything should be instant and effortless.

We also think that we have the *right* to those things,[1] but this is because the powers that be (whether Authorities or authorities) are also working to satisfy the same basic desires as the rest of us. They want to be thought of as dealing in the sweet stuff themselves. Rights feel sweet, and they are easy to sell. They do not necessarily depend on effort or input, they are givens – freebies, in fact – which we obviously *deserve* just because we're alive. There is something akin to the thinking of the pre-revolutionary French aristocracy in that, I feel.

But isn't that thinking the remnant, the pretty dream, of an individualistic world in which population growth appeared to be manageable (to most of us, at least) and growth, commercialism and unbounded enterprise were seen as totally positive forces? Now, as we finally recognise that selfish demands on the world's resources have had a devastating effect on matters like climate and biodiversity (as well as on our waistlines), we are also beginning to realise that to save the planet we will have to act together. We will have to work in concert over all kinds of issues, from targets on carbon emissions to single-use plastic bags. Some individual 'freedoms' will just have to be curtailed, however liberating it felt on a personal level to live as spontaneously as we liked.

We may be getting it, but we are still some way off understanding that self-gratifying behaviour (which can come in surprising guises) is just as bad for our species' mental health environment as it is for our physical environment, and that we must also act more in concert, as socially connected beings, to help save our mental health.

Perhaps we need less of 'I', 'myself' and 'me' and more of 'we', 'us' and 'they'. Although this may sound as though I'm contradicting my earlier claim that we should be able to achieve more individual power and control over our mental health, that isn't really the case. It's complicated, but basically it's about prioritising personal *agency* over personal *preferences*.

---

1   Advertisers are some of the worst offenders when it comes to creating a sense of entitlement to 'goodies'. There is even an advert that tells us we shouldn't have to choose between domestic heating – which is just about the most important and fundamental thing achieved by mankind, after sufficient food supplies – and a skiing holiday for the family. Heating is a boring given, whereas *fun* is what we should be entitled to. Eh, what? Am I missing something here?

Addicted to self

For so long we have been handmaidens to our own emotional desires, feeding them as if they were little gods. As with any addiction, we have ended up bloated and ever more selfish, without any consideration for the impact we're having on others or on the outside world and how it functions in general. As long as *I* have what *I* desire and what feels good to *me* – lifestyle, opinions, emotions, whatever – that is so much more important than concerning myself with any impact I might also be having on the planet or on my family, friends, neighbours and fellow planet dwellers.

Quite possibly, the ultimate expression of our fixation with the self is the selfie itself. It is also a very good model of what is happening in and to society. As we turn the lens on ourselves, we are literally turning our backs on the outside world and cradling ourselves in our own hands, looking into our own eyes and simpering until we like the look – babying ourselves in our palms.

Recently I went to the National Gallery to look at the paintings. I could hardly get near them for the slow lava flow of tourists taking images of themselves standing in front of (and largely blocking out) the rather more outstanding images in the gallery's collection. Not only did the inconvenience to other visitors not seem to trouble them in the least, but also apparently it didn't occur to the (mostly young) tourists to experience the paintings first hand by simply looking at them. And there, in that seemingly harmless piece of self-absorption, is a perfect example of the connection between the immediate sweetness of selfies and mental self-harm. If I am everywhere, in everything I look at, then the world is going to be ever less about the other and ever more about me.

It's that metaphorical as well as literal focus on the self which has been identified as being behind a lot of negative mental states. I will be going into more detail on this later in the book, but the disproportionate focus on I, myself and me that arises in a selfie culture has been closely associated with greater than normal levels of depression and anxiety, and even with suicidal thoughts. That is a sad thought in itself, but there is also a solution contained within it.

Previous generations who experienced life from a (literally) more objective standpoint had the advantage over mobile phone era youngsters, because once there was you and then there was the outside world (with needs, desires and rights that were different from your own), which you were trying to make sense of in some way, and that might include capturing its 'reality' in a photo. Now, you take the photo with yourself in it, often modifying it in some way as you're taking it – which is really a form of personal editing – and then you're likely to post it on a social media site, which is another way of reflecting your own image (in both senses) and lifestyle. So, how and when do you ever delete yourself from being your first consideration? It's like being in one of those halls of mirrors that keep on reflecting more and more images of you, yourself and you.

For many younger people, the so-called 'outside world' – mostly a brain's fiction anyway – is fast becoming even more of a fiction. And it's a fiction that can't be called out because, without shared experiences (oversharing on social media after the event is entirely different and demands that the validation is on your own terms), how can anyone be sure of their ground? In a world of one, how do I know what is me and what is outside me? I love the brilliantly surreal 'spider baby' episode in *Father Ted* ('Good Luck, Father Ted') in which Ted attempts to explain the difference between dreams and reality to Father Dougal using a hand-drawn diagram. It captures the near impossibility of the task better than I ever could!

On a darker, more tragic and terrifying note, a young man named Robert Bragg recently described his experience of being involved in the gang-related stabbing of he didn't know how many people in the following way: 'It's just one of them things: you wake up, you have your breakfast, you stab someone. It's mad because we're not actually thinking about damaging a life. We don't think we're going to kill you.'[2] Does your blood run cold at the sheer lack of humanity implied here? There's no real sense here that 'other' has an actual existence and that his behaviour towards 'other' will affect that existence, perhaps for ever. This is what happens when we haven't learned to think and observe outside the box of our own heads.[3] Fortunately, that young man has moved on and is now in a much better place.

But how could someone whose brain is still in the development stage anyway be expected to have a truly balanced view of life when so much of their viewing is of themselves? In such a barely real world, how are we supposed to know genuine friend from online imposter, genuine cause for unhappiness from social media generated emotional confection – or, it appears, taking breakfast from taking life?

Having said all that, time isn't going to go backwards and technology isn't going to be un-invented (much of it is quite simply brilliant, so we wouldn't want to un-invent it). Again, I think the real problem lies in the ways it is being used to promote I, myself and me. It's that obsessive self-interest that is the problem, not the equipment used to endorse and support it.

Self-absorption has been around for quite a while (*Hamlet,* anyone?), but I can't be the only person who secretly suspects that ever since we have been encouraged to express ourselves and talk about feelings, the problem with our mental health seems to have got worse. Not that I think talking is the problem per se – there are many reasons why talking may be a very good thing for mental health (more on this later, especially in Chapter 4). It's the talking about *feelings* that seems to have been the catalyst.

Why? Because talking about feelings is generally taken to mean *my* feelings, which are just about the most individualistic things out there. Self-pleasuring again. What could possibly be sweeter than talking about *my* feelings, *my* sense of injustice, *my* woes, *my* being misunderstood, *my* hard times and so on?

---

3   There are so many teenage murders happening now, often for no clear reason. It seems that decades of watching animations of various sorts as well as imaginary scenarios in films and video games, together with an acceptance that the 'hot' emotions of the moment matter more than any rational thoughts, have left youngsters unable to comprehend that 'real life' is out there, and that some things genuinely are forever – like death. At some deep level it appears that there are young people who think that death is just another thing you can rewind, time shift or simply walk away from while ordering enchiladas – or more likely wraps of another kind. I will be going into the connection between drugs and states of unreality in Chapter 7 because it's hugely important to mental health.

One of the great beauties of feelings is that no one else can ever deny them (this 'truth' is now seemingly woven into British law: if you *feel* offended then someone *has* genuinely harmed you), even though we don't really have a valid definition of what a feeling is – a lack I will be attempting to address. One thing I'm already pretty sure of, though, is that like many of the sweet substances I'm going to be writing about, the empty calories contained in some feelings have been helping our sense of self-importance to grow fat.

There seems to be an absolute acceptance that if we could just get everyone talking about their feelings, then all would be well. I think we need to be a bit more open-minded (and intellectually curious) and start to question this largely unsubstantiated assumption. I've come across many a client who was hugely eloquent about their various emotional states but none the mentally sounder for it.

I introduced the word resilience earlier, suggesting that it was our number one defence against mental health problems. There have been many studies which have shown that having a resilient personality is the key to overcoming the stresses and challenges of life without succumbing to mental anguish. I will be saying more about what goes into the making of a resilient personality in Chapter 10, but for now I just want to observe that a large part of being resilient is having the ability to look beyond the self – beyond I, myself, me – and my feelings. It's about appreciating and being curious about the wider world; it means being nosy about, not the self, but life itself.

It's also a form of robust mental exercise, which we're going to need if we want to compensate for the hothouse internalising lifestyle

which has left us with some emotional flabbiness. And, as with our physical weight problems, we can either wait for the powers that be to step in, pathologise the problem and offer us medical solutions, or we can take a long hard look at how we came to be like this in the first place, and then take steps – literal and metaphorical – to trim down any excess from our self-pleasuring past and start to build resilient muscle in preparation for the future.

Chapter 2

A fixation on fixing life?

I'm aware that much of what I'm going to say in this book won't go down well with some, but I don't think that is a good enough reason not to say it, especially as I detect a little emotional obesity in the choirs of sensitive voices which sing, 'You can't say *that*!' There's rather a lot of Violet Elizabeth Bott about them – she of the 'I'll scream and scream and scream until I'm sick, and I can' threat which does so much to upset William Brown's mental wellbeing.

As I said at the start, there's been too much pussyfooting around sensitivities, and we need to consider *all* possibilities when it comes to cause and effect in mental health matters. The self-determined fragility of individuals who shriek 'Na, na, na' with their fingers in their ears whenever something gets said that they don't approve of, is very much part of the problem rather than a response to it.

We've reached a critical state and lives are being lost or compromised, so what I'm about to suggest should in no way be seen as undermining or contradicting that fact. But I have also implied that we are in a situation of our own making when I observed in the introduction that life events which at other times may have been little more than nuisances or inconveniences can now be the cause of genuine psychic pain. I want to stress the word *genuine* because I'm not suggesting that young people are making up their distress – they do genuinely feel it.

However, science tells us that the observer affects the observed (Schrödinger's pesky cat either is or isn't the evidence for that!). In a selfie world in which youngsters are turning the spotlight on themselves, they are perhaps impacting on their own states of mind – that is, experiencing symptoms they might otherwise not have done, largely because they're focusing so closely on themselves.[1]

It's worth taking a look at a recent survey to see how self-determined fragility might well be affecting our perception of what is going on.[2] The survey was carried out by the NHS, and looked into the psychiatric records of 10,000 young people, not all of whom had asked for help with mental problems. They found that the proportion of under 16s who had experienced any disorder (including anxiety and depression) had gone up from 11.4% in 1999 to 13.6% in 2017. The rise was described as being smaller than anticipated.

Other findings were that 17–19-year-old girls were two-thirds more likely than younger girls (and twice as likely as similar aged boys) to experience poor mental health. There was also a big gap between the rise in referrals to Child and Adolescent Mental Health Services (CAMHS) and the number of children who were found to have a diagnosable mental disorder. The NHS deduced from these findings that a large part of the increase was down to more people looking for help, rather than more people actually experiencing mental health problems. This leaves us with the big question: why are more young people reporting that they are unwell?

Some possible answers might be:

- Children and parents are better at spotting problems.
- There is self-reporting of symptoms as disorders, even when not formally diagnosable as such.
- There are blurred lines between clinical and subclinical symptoms (i.e. confusion between anxiety as a reaction to circumstances and a permanently anxious state or disorder).

To sum up: although there is some uncertainty over the actual scale of the increase in mental health problems, there is a small but

---

1   Psychotherapist and activist Jo Watson and psychologist Lucy Johnstone of the campaign group A Disorder for Everyone (AD4E) suggest that the 'insidious colonisation of counselling and psychotherapy language and practice by medical-model diagnosis' can cause iatrogenic harm to someone experiencing mental distress. See Catherine Jackson, Who needs a diagnosis?, *Therapy Today* (8 February 2019). Available at: https://www.bacp.co.uk/bacp-journals/therapy-today/2019/february-2019/who-needs-a-diagnosis. 'Iatrogenic' refers to illness caused by medical examination or treatment.

2   NHS, *Mental Health of Children and Young People in England* (2017). Available at: https://digital.nhs.uk/data-and-information/publications/statistical/mental-health-of-children-and-young-people-in-england/2017/2017.

measurable increase, and girls in particular seem to be experiencing a decline in their feelings of wellbeing.

Is this evidence that there is something going on here that could be classified as self-determined fragility? And might there also be a determination to see stats where stats don't really exist – sort of Schrödinger's stats?[3] I think all that can be said confidently is that there are quite a few young people (actual numbers probably unknowable) who, at a time when they could be enjoying the limitless health and optimism of youth, are feeling miserable, uninspired and pointless.[4] Which, if nothing else, is immeasurably sad.

Even if part of the problem is that young people (and girls especially) are identifying their experiences as depressing, traumatic, anxiety provoking and so on, when once they may have regarded them as an inevitable part of any normal life in this vale of tears, that is still a problem. Something has swung too far in the opposite direction if we've gone from being able to tolerate the pretty awful (wars, industrialisation, rural poverty, etc.) to not being able to tolerate life in a world that includes many of the material benefits that past generations would have seen as the answers to their prayers.

I don't want to bang on about this too much, but in the course of this week I've randomly read short articles on the lives of J. R. R. Tolkien, Gerald Finzi and Charlotte Brontë – and what tragedies they experienced! Tolkien lost both parents when he was a boy, and later, when serving in the trenches, all but one of the friends he had fought alongside died. Finzi lost his father at the age of 8, and then his beloved music teacher and all three of his brothers in the First World War. Brontë lost her mother at the age of 5, two sisters in

---

3   According to an American scientist, machine learning techniques are causing huge problems for research science. Dr Genevera Allen of Rice University, Houston, says that software is now identifying patterns that exist only in datasets and not in the real world, and the results are only occasionally reproducible. It has been suggested that up to 85% of biomedical research is wasted effort and that many experiments are not sufficiently well designed to ensure that scientists don't only get the results they are looking for. See Pallab Ghosh, AAAS: machine learning 'causing science crisis', *BBC News* (16 February 2019). Available at: https://www.bbc.co.uk/news/science-environment-47267081.

4   See, for example, Henry Bodkin, Tens of thousands of UK children have PTSD due to bullying and violence, Lancet study finds, *The Telegraph* (22 February 2019). Available at: https://www.telegraph.co.uk/news/2019/02/22/tens-thousands-uk-children-have-ptsd-due-bullying-violence-lancet; Ed Southgate, Freshers declaring mental illness up 73% in 4 years, *The Times* (22 February 2019); Kat Lay, Self-harm hospital admissions for children double in 6 years, *The Times* (23 February 2019).

childhood, two more as an adult, and her brother was both alco-holic and drug addicted.

These cases weren't particularly unusual back in the day, but now any one of these losses or traumatic experiences would be viewed as a reason for mental health problems. And, dare I suggest it, the *lack* of a traumatised response might be seen as problematic, rather than the other way around.[5]

Of course, they were all deeply affected by what had happened to them, and in their respective art forms each explored themes around innocence and loss. (Tolkien believed that fairy tales are the real stories of life, and that the essence of a fairy tale is the happy ending. After bad events, good will prevail – which is pretty amaz-ing, given his experiences.) I am not suggesting that people in the past were less sensitive to suffering than people nowadays (that way lies a very suspect kind of emotional imperialism and superiority), but I am suggesting that they may have something to teach us about how to deal with what life throws at us. Or, to put it another way, they may have something to teach us about being better adjusted.

Because we seem to have lost the art of being well-adjusted. The phrase carries the understanding that life ain't perfect, that stuff happens and that we have to roll with the blows on occasion. That is to say, we should know how to react flexibly in life, which is another way of saying *with resilience*. We should be well-adjusted to the lives we end up having to lead – especially when, despite all we think we *should* be entitled to, life goes its own sweet way without reference to what we personally want or need.[6]

And that is getting harder and harder all the time, because perfec-tionism and perfectibility (both of which mitigate against the openness to experience at the heart of resilience) are the order of the day. Tolkien, Finzi, Brontë; they could all shape their experi-ences and their pain into art, escaping the horrors of what had

---

5   A case study published in *Therapy Today* contains the following lines: 'but I noted a disconnection between her traumatic experiences and the emotions she expressed. In counselling, we worked on recognising and expressing physical sensations in the present moment and connecting them to her emotions.' In other words, in counselling at least, it is understood that there is an *appropriate* response to trauma, and that a person's responses must be corrected if they don't have that emotionally correct reaction to their experiences. See Cate Harding-Jones, Counselling survivors of sex trafficking, *Therapy Today* (23 February 2019). Available at: https://www.bacp.co.uk/bacp-journals/therapy-today/2019/february-2019.

6   Can I possibly be alone in thinking that the expression 'my best life' is both profoundly delusional and totally nauseating?

happened to them through doorways into the more magical lands of the imagination which they could order and control. But ordinary, daily, imperfect life still carried on in much more mundane ways; they simply got on with it in relative, outward calm.

However, if they had thought they were entitled to expect lives full of happiness, wellbeing and physical beauty, to name but a few things which rank highly in the 'needs' and expectations of many teenagers today, perhaps, instead of translating their emotions into successful art, they would have realised how unhappy they were and spent their time in therapy instead. Just wondering ...

If I have got a point here, and young people are suffering not so much from worse experiences than their forebears as from a greater mismatch between their expectations and their experiences, then it's necessary to get to the causes of that mismatch before the outcomes can be challenged. Either the disparity stems from a valid set of expectations coming up against experiences that need to be corrected for, or it's the other way around.

As individuals, we can learn to control for one of these scenarios, but it will be a whole lot harder to control for the other. Or to put it more simply: it's easier to adjust our expectations than it is to change the world.

Chapter 3

In which sugar and resilience come together ...

... in a ground-breaking study known as the marshmallow experiment, which originated in work carried out in the 1960s and 1970s by Walter Mischel, professor of psychology at Stanford University in the United States.

Although some of the findings of the marshmallow experiment have been critiqued (not entirely convincingly to my mind) by a more recent study,[1] the fundamental behaviours which are relevant to us here still apply.

Briefly, the marshmallow experiment found that children who, in the course of research to ascertain the age when self-control can be exercised (they were then 3 or 4), were able to reject a single proffered marshmallow in favour of the promise of two future marshmallows, became much more resilient adults than those who were not. To their astonishment, Mischel and his team found that these children went on to be happier, healthier (mentally and physically), wealthier and more successful adults in every respect than their peers who had not been able to reject the immediate reward – or, as it's more commonly known, delay gratification. Angela Lee Duckworth, a psychologist working with Mischel's fundamental premise, has gone as far as saying that the ability to delay gratification is a far better predictor of academic success than IQ alone.[2]

The more recent research by Watts and colleagues has questioned how important class is to the whole equation, but whether or not we buy into that, the techniques and strategies used to delay gratification by those who can certainly offer some very interesting insights

---

1   See Tyler W. Watts, Greg J. Duncan and Haonan Quan, Revisiting the marshmallow test: a conceptual replication investigating links between early delay of gratification and later outcomes, *Psychological Science* 29(7) (2018): 1159–1177.

2   See Jonah Lehrer, Don't! The secret of self-control, *The New Yorker* (11 May 2009). Available at: https://www.newyorker.com/magazine/2009/05/18/dont-2.

into how our brains work to give us self-control, whatever our social status, and also some very interesting connections to the present mental health crisis.

If you're reading this then you're probably an adult, so marshmallows may not be the hottest temptation you can imagine (maybe they aren't for kids either, it was the 1960s). Perhaps for you there are more alluring possibilities: alcohol, Big Macs, a credit card-fuelled shopping spree, an online casino – you get the picture. In the business, such things are called 'hot stimuli' – material things, substances and behaviours that go straight past your higher thinking (and your self-control) and ram into the emotional nuclear fuel bunker that is your amygdala, where they cause an explosion of deep pleasure and satiation.

Which lasts approximately as long as the explosion. And then you want more …

I once gave a talk to parents of anxious pre-A level sixth-formers at a very prestigious and academic girls' school in London. I described the mechanisms behind resilience as I understood them and talked about Walter Mischel's work. They understood that self-control and delayed gratification could be helpful in building up resistance to the immediate demands of emotionalism (something that teenage girls are prone to in particular), but one mother was left with a big question and came up to me after the talk had finished.

'If what you say is right,' she questioned, 'then why does my daughter have a mental health problem, anorexia, when she so obviously is in control of her appetite and is practised at delaying gratification pretty much all of the time?'

It was a very good question, and fortunately there is a very good answer to it. A hot stimulus can be many different things, but in the case of someone with an eating disorder it can be one of two more or less opposite things. With bulimia (or gorging behaviour) the stimulus (or compelling emotional motivation) is cramming food in, but with anorexia it is the control of starving the body. What that poor confused mum had to deal with was a daughter who was actually giving in to the hot stimulus of starvation, whereas delaying gratification for her would mean putting off the emotional satisfaction that comes with starvation in favour of the 'more sensible' option of eating.

Usually, the stimulus is a clearer indulgence of appetite – being a lovely sweet thing that sits there either begging us to 'eat me, eat me', 'drink me, drink me' or emotionally to 'feel me, feel me', 'experience me, experience me'.

Now, let's get back to the mechanics of how delaying the gratification of those appetites works ...

What is a man?

What is a man

If his chief good and market of his time

Be but to sleep and feed? A beast, no more.

Sure, he that made us with such large discourse,

Looking before and after, gave us not

That capability and godlike reason

To fust in us unused.

Hamlet, **IV, iv.**

Shakespeare is generally right about a lot of things to do with human behaviour, and what he says here about how we come to be human is particularly relevant to mental health today. We become human when we look before and after – to the past and the future.

What Mischel found in his experiment was that those kids who could delay gratification (i.e. wait to gain an extra marshmallow rather than scoffing the one in front of them straight away) were the ones who were best at distracting themselves, perhaps by looking out of the window, sitting on their hands or whistling. In effect, they were 'cooling' the effect of the scorching hot stimulus of the marshmallow.

That may seem like an obvious strategy to you, but it's actually a pretty sophisticated one. It involves being much more than a beast; only rarely do other animals delay gratification of their own accord. It involves looking backwards and forwards, it involves self-determination and it involves taking more interest in the outside world than in your own immediate emotional desires. In other words, it involves all the skills necessary to be resilient through life.

Looking backwards and forwards in time suggests having context and overview, plus the ability to see yourself as part of a bigger process, as a figure in a bigger landscape which has other actors in it. The child will have memories of other occasions when they needed to wait for something. They will believe that the strategies which distracted them then will work again now to take their mind off whatever it is that is so very, very appealing. And they will also have (and this is hugely important) a pretty strong belief that what is promised will actually come to pass in the future – that the second marshmallow is a genuine offer and worth the wait.

These kids actually have teeny-weeny timelines with teeny-weeny narratives inside their heads, and they remember the past as a way of predicting the future.[3] Theirs is a world in which self-agency (they can control what happens to them), consistency (they can believe in what is said to them) and outward orientation or interest in the outside world (research has shown that babies who are clingy from the start are less distractible and more focused on their own sensations[4]) are already in place at a very young age. Shakespeare is right, as usual. Having mental maps or charts across time really does make us godlike in our ability to manage ourselves and, as a consequence, our lives.[5]

---

3   On the role of memory in making us human, Alison George cites the case of a patient who had an impaired episodic memory after a motorcycle accident – 'he could remember facts, but not personal experiences'. However, as well as impairing his ability to recall the past, the injury had also compromised his ability to imagine the future. Imaging studies have shown that similar brain activity occurs when we remember past events and plan future ones. Eleanor Maguire of University College London suggests that the key is being able to generate 'scenes in the mind's eye'. If we are unable to remember previous experiences, our capacity to make well-thought-through decisions deteriorates. George theorises that 'being able to picture the past [may have] enabled us to imagine the future, and therefore plan – one of the complex cognitive feats that stand humans apart from many other species'. See Alison George, Memory special: do we even know what memory is for?, *New Scientist* (24 October 2018). Available at: https://www.newscientist.com/article/mg24032010-500-memory-special-do-we-even-know-what-memory-is-for.

4   John Bowlby's work on attachment (1969) showed that babies who could rely on the physical and emotional availability of their primary carers became more self-reliant, curious and adventurous than babies who felt more insecure and were either more clingy or more indifferent to everything as a result.

5   Navigation of time and space, which is what both timelines and maps represent, is the job of a brain area called the hippocampus. But it also does another job, one which is almost identical in many ways, and that is to remember what we have done, where we have been and when.

This brings me back to my starting point, because we now have a sketchy outline of what *good* mental health is all about. It's essentially about being resilient – as long as resilience is taken to mean resilience at the deepest level, as a brain behaviour, rather than as a media-generated sound bite. It is not so much about being strong or empowered, as about being able to avoid the temptation to give in to our appetites (which can be to indulge in the sweetness of emotionalism or sentimentality as well as junk food, drink or drugs) or to collapse under stress. It means being able to fail at something and pick ourselves up, dust ourselves down and start all over again. And it means having the strength to carry others with us, in addition to keep going ourselves, when the going gets tough.

To do all these things also means having in place mental timelines which take us from the past into the future, and brains which can make ethical and emotional judgements about any decisions we might make. (Science has shown that individuals with brain damage that affects emotional aspects of behaviour find it very difficult to make decisions at all, leaving them almost paralysed with indecision.[6])

Also necessary to resilience is a resistance to making the self numero uno in planning and decision-making. Although this ability is all part and parcel of seeing the bigger picture, it's worth really putting the spotlight on the huge benefits that come to mental health from ditching I, myself and me thinking in favour of we, us, and they. And, of course, putting others more into the frame is also an outcome of having that other resilience-critical skill – being endlessly curious about the outside world and life in general.

A focus on finding things outside ourselves fascinating (like those young children distracted by scenes outside the window) helps to damp down the hot stimulus of inner sensations, or what we are encouraged to call 'feelings',[7] and that can only be a good thing in the present highly emotional climate. But the ability to tweak that focus and to make our own sensations into objective curiosities, which we can observe as if they are external to ourselves, also helps

---

6   Claire Salmond, David Menon, Doris Chatfield, John Pickard and Barbara Sahakian, Deficits in decision-making in head injury survivors, *Journal of Neurotrauma* 22(6) (2005): 613–622.

7   I'm coming to the whole 'trouble with feelings' issue very soon.

with mental health problems; in my opinion, it is the element in both mindfulness and cognitive-behavioural therapy (CBT) which is the most beneficial.

To tidy all of that into a neat, minimal list encompassing what good mental health consists of is:

- Seeing yourself as part of a bigger picture.
- Having the ability to remember the past and predict the future.
- Having confidence in a consistent, stable world (it doesn't have to be a particularly good one).
- Having curiosity about that world.
- Prioritising things other than personal feelings/emotions (although understanding them is important).

Note: It is not about happiness, positive mental outlook, growth mindset or anything as 'now' as that. Some of these outcomes might be both useful and lovely to have, but they are not the foundation stones of good mental health.

There, a nice tidy summary of what it takes to be resilient, which in turn results in good mental health. All that's left is to find out how to become a person with those attributes. A doddle.

Why not begin at the end?

Chapter 4

Hot stuff and cool reason

Did I really write those words: 'prioritising things other than personal feelings/emotions'? I know I added the rider, 'although understanding them is important', but even so! What could possibly be more important than feelings and emotions?

Enough with all the punctuation and laden sarcasm. All the same, I hope you grasp the implications of my opening paragraph; I think I'm going to have a battle on my hands to persuade recent generations of the newly emotionally literate that our personal inner experiences are not the only things going on in the world, and nor are they necessarily the most important or best guides in life. In fact, it's possible that feelings will turn out to have been partially sighted guides with such limited vision that they are responsible for myopically leading us into the mental health quagmire in which we're being swallowed.

So, to the 'trouble with feelings', which are just another brain behaviour, of course – but with attitude.

A very simple way to think about the human brain is to see it as a traffic management system. There is a lot of flow as vast numbers of vehicles have to get to many and various destinations: destinations which are often determined by the content of their cargoes. They may be carrying materials that are essential for the basic functioning of the community or for more specialised and sophisticated requirements, and then there is transport for communications and for social purposes. In brain terms, we're talking motor and sensory functions, understanding, memory, speech, language and so on. But there are also vehicles on the road which, although occasionally used for work, aren't specifically designed for it and are used for other, possibly nefarious, purposes, too. We'll come back to them later.

In order to run smoothly, everything within that overall system needs to be managed by subsystems of signage, lineage, lights and roundabouts, so that all the movements coordinate. And the whole lot has to be overseen and controlled by traffic headquarters, which is run by a cool, calm, Greek goddess-like functionary. Without this oversight and control all hell breaks loose. The system depends on being alert to the needs and movements of every element, and on strict regulation which ensures that individual priorities are sidelined in favour of the functioning of the whole. It all breaks down if any part fails to act in concert with the rest, which in functional terms can mean that brain areas dealing with bodily movement and sensory matters can be as much impacted by any ensuing chaos as those dealing with mental and emotional matters.

Of course, there are always going to be a few outliers in any set-up, and who hasn't at some stage been pushed off the road by a raging primitive hothead, thrashing a hot hatch to the limit as they squeal around corners, blast through red lights or overtake like a lunatic on blind bends? These characters are going to get to where they want to go, no, *need* to go (that very important disused industrial estate where they plan to show the world how important they are) just because … well, *just because, okay*? And you're not going to get in their way. *Get it, loser?*

Never mind the cars that crash in their wake, and the fact that the whole of the A777 and the centre of town are now in a state of vehicular chaos, and no one but them is currently going anywhere. Even the emergency vehicles needed to clean up their mess are caught in the jam.

I don't want to overdo the traffic metaphor, because once you get down into the detail it doesn't quite work; ultimately, a brain is a brain, and it works just like – a brain. But I do want to create a hopefully memorable image to help explain the often apparently pointless and frequently thoughtless and inconsiderate behaviour of a relatively primitive part of our brain called the amygdala which operates within our limbic system. The limbic system is part of the brain's overall and necessary traffic, as it is involved in fundamental behaviours and responses that we need for survival. The amygdala's role in this subsystem of the brain is also essential, as it deals with unsophisticated, single-issue (but strong) emotions like anger, fear, anxiety and pleasure, which are some of our most instinctive and primitive reactions to experiences of threat and comfort.

However, when it comes to complex modern societies – which involve lots of people and lots of competing needs and desires – the brain, like a traffic system, needs to deal with more than one simple set of demands. And just like those hot-hatch hotheads, the emotions (be they positive or negative) that the amygdala deals in can be the primitive drivers of pretty uncontrolled and selfish behaviour. Only too often it is behaviour which prevents other brain traffic from running smoothly and it can result in, at best, behavioural and emotional imbalance and, at worst, chaos – unless these particular crazy hotheads get reined in by that cool, goddess-like functionary, our prefrontal cortex.[1]

One subtask of the amygdala is adding emotional resonance, or power, to memories and causing them to 'stick'. Fearful memories seem to be among the stickiest of all emotional memories, meaning they don't slip away as easily as pleasant everyday memories. While we may forget the gentle canal-side walk that we took one balmy summer evening, we absolutely can't shake off the gut-squeezing memory of the chilly night we heard footsteps following us along it.

It may even make us a bit angry looking back on it because there is a very close relationship between fear and anger. Like fraternal twins they hang around together and back each other up, so although anger can be scary in itself, it is also nature's way of making fear less, well, frightening. Anger pumps us up for action even when we're feeling scared; likewise, fear can be a useful limiter on anger, stopping us from acting out angrily in the face of the massive guy who has just nicked our parking space.

On the other hand, letting rip regardless, just because we're so very angry that we don't give a monkey's any more – boy, can that feel good! And we don't even have the bother of considering what we should do next; we just get down and dirty and *do* it. Anger, red mist, rage, all driven by our amygdalae (plural, we have two), can feel pretty empowering, not to say orgasmic at times – which is perhaps why so many of us find really angry heroes really sexy.

To return to our hothead hot-hatch guys, are they really any kind of hero – sexy or otherwise – or are they just selfish short-term pleasure seekers, driven (literally and metaphorically) by some deep-seated anger to override (again, both literally and metaphorically) the

---

1   While the amygdala lies deep within the brain, the prefrontal area evolved relatively recently and lies just behind our (big) foreheads. Its functions are modern, complex and sophisticated, dealing with matters like planning, decision-making, self-control and advanced social behaviour.

other traffic in the brain as they satisfy their more primitive urges? Urges which are frequently triggered at the deepest level, not by pleasure as such, but by some supremely sticky but disproportionately represented memories which are attached to past fears and injustices. This has certainly been the case for many of the prisoners I've worked with (some of them genuinely red-hot hot-hatch drivers), who have all combined anger with deep-rooted fear, and both of those with a complete and almost visceral disregard for anything but their own immediate desires and requirements. The scared and confused little boy beaten by his dad for not getting his beers quickly enough becomes the strutting, drug-dealing, twoccing, joyriding king of the estate.

Aren't real heroes supposed to take care of others, to put others first and to act for the greater good? In this context, it's the cool Grecian goddess traffic managers with their sophisticated systems who oversee the whole network, and can take past behaviours, future probabilities and needs into account, who are the true heroes. It's these so-called executives of our brains – located in our prefrontal lobes – which, by taking *all* of the traffic into account, allow our brains (and our bodies) to function healthily and effectively.

Well, mostly, because actually neither amygdala nor prefrontal area is properly functional on its own; it's the balance, the interplay, between the two that makes for really good mental health. After all, if the prefrontal cortex is unable to recognise the amygdala's more colourful impulses, nor its likely behaviours, how can it predict and prevent unwanted ones or make good decisions about the future? It has to at least understand the brain's feelings and emotions. Equally, if the amygdala is too forceful and overwhelming, and destroys everything that gets in its way, well, it won't have a world in which to operate (or lord it over). They need each other.

Ah, yes, I have just used that word again – feelings, the 'brain's feelings' – although I only did so to bring it back into the argument. I would prefer to say 'the brain's sensations' or even 'the body's sensations', which is really more to the point as that is where we actually experience things like elation, fear, anger and so on (check yourself out). In fact, our brains have few sensations, which is why they can be operated on without pain. However, their traffic systems have such a confusion of crossroads, loops and intersections, all carrying information about physical sensations and mental interpretations backwards and forwards, that without helpful scrutiny and intervention from above (i.e. our Grecian goddess), neither side really knows where or what the sensation is. It's a pushmi-pullyu kind of situation, and as such I don't think our obsession with feelings will be ultimately taking us anywhere.

I may be in a minority of one, but as the rest of the emotionally woke world is now constantly urging feelings on everyone, it's important to understand what we mean by the word. I want to explain why I think an overemphasis on feelings is part of the mental health problem, rather than being (as so many others seem to think) the solution to it.

Perhaps we should blame Shirley Bassey for popularising the idea that feelings are valuable interpretations of our inner sensations, or perhaps post-Freudian therapy with its endless incantation of, 'So, tell me, how does that make you feel?' Originally the word meant experiencing something through the sense of touch, and only over time did it come to mean an inner sensation relating to emotions. And that rather tends to mirror our journey from having had externally orientated relationships with the world – ones in which we reached out towards it, or at the very least recognised its impact on us through our alert and outward-seeking sensors/senses – to where we've arrived at now: having almost wholly internalised relationships which depend instead on our construing the world and its impact on us through our self-generated certainties. Or to put it another way: 'I don't take my lead from the world because the world is only of importance to me, through me, and my own sensations/feelings.'

Our primary sensation is now an internal affair. It is personal – it is to do with I, myself and me. Where once feelings involved abundant feedback from the outside world, in addition to our emotional responses to it,[2] we now seem to start with the emotional response. And even then it's a response to a world we've largely created in our own heads (see the earlier references to selfies).

However, for any certainty I may be *feeling*, there is nothing demonstrable or provable involved in my sensation, and nor for all any of us knows (although fMRI scans are getting close) is any mutual experience involved either. There may be as many variations on feelings as there are people on the planet, but we give them common

---

2   People were much more in touch with it through exposure to weather, physical labour, direct communication, having to travel in more social and exposed ways and so on.

names which we're supposed to understand and even empathise with. There can't be too much argument about what a table is, or a blow to the stomach for that matter. But a feeling such as sorrow, humiliation or emotional pain – how can anyone say with any real certainty that they know what another person means by these words, much less understand how intense or troublesome their sensations around them are?

Why then, if they are such shifty things, should feelings have come to more or less dominate our understanding of mental and emotional health to such an extent that they are now used to establish harm in law? We don't expect the entire outside world to respect our personal and individual discomfort around things which affect our senses, such as smells or noises. Objections to violations of personal comfort in these areas have to involve many people, not just one, and they tend to be regarded as a balancing act or a question of preferences. You may not like that rap music, but others do. Equally, someone can deeply offend my nose on the London Underground, but that is highly unlikely to lead to a prosecution.

Offend an individual someone's feelings though, especially around certain key issues, and that is a different matter. Feelings count, especially when they are hurt ones. After all, whoever heard of someone being given money from the public purse for generating good feelings? Why, oh why, might this be?

I believe that it's partly a question of individualism: the inner personal experience is becoming culturally more important than the shared experience, even if the inner experience is in no way provable. On top of that, completely unmediated and unrestrained by the outward-leaning, emotion-cooling prefrontal cortex, there is the impact of a wonderful explosion of raw emotion in the amygdala. Hurt feelings involve strong emotions because they are the result of what are regarded as attacks on the sense of self. If the self is culturally all-important, then fear is involved: I might be annihilated. And with fear, as we have seen, comes anger. (In cultures where there is less focus on the self there is less fear, and so a greater ability to shrug off matters like personal criticism.[3])

We're getting into that sugar rush of intense emotions – of rectitude, anger, hurt and injustice (see *Hamlet* for the best display of these out there). And it's all washed down with chasers of I, myself and me: 'I'm so alone in all this – why should this be happening to me?' As I have already observed, there is a sweet and complementary relationship here: the empty calories of feelings like these really do help a rather distorted sense of self-importance to grow fat, and our heightened sense of damaged self enjoys a certain kind of sweetness in the hurt. It's a weird form of self-pleasuring self-harm.

And, boy, the amygdala has a whale of a time with all this emotional self-indulgence! It careers all over the place, recklessly overtaking everything in its path, to the absolute detriment of the smooth running of the brain. But what about our Grecian goddess? Where is the prefrontal cortex to balance out the hot emotion of the (perhaps genuine) grievance with some calm reflection and a sense of the bigger picture (remember how important that is)? Why isn't it doing a better job? From politics and advertising to TV programmes, social media and children's play, so much of the narrative is driven by aggression, anger and passionate feelings – sometimes referred to as 'vibrancy', 'creative tension' and other such euphemisms.

This brings me back to advertising, because advertisers know a thing or two about playing on people's emotions: from the use of 'hot' language – nothing is ever uncomfortable, nice or interesting; it's always heartbreaking, traumatising, amazing, awesome or guaranteed to blow you away and change your life forever – to its determination to portray a desirable life as being full-on, polychromatic, playground-level fun rather than a thing of order, commitment and routine. We have all been subjected to the *zeitgeist* marketing of 'super-sized', 'here' and 'now'. We have all been sold the pleasure to be had from instant, sweet and strong, as well as the

3   See *The Significance Delusion*, p. 128. See also: 'Giving and Receiving Criticism' business training by Boundless Communications at https://courses.lumenlearning.com/boundless-communications/chapter/giving-and-receiving-criticism; and Batja Mesquita of the Catholic University of Leuven: 'If you live in a culture where an emotion like anger is viewed as disturbing and selfish, you will not be rewarded for expressing it, and over time you may even cease to feel it.' Quoted in Linda Geddes, Self-mastery can be yours with three pillars of emotional wisdom, *New Scientist* (2 January 2016). Available at: https://www.newscientist.com/article/mg22930540-800-self-mastery-can-be-yours-with-three-pillars-of-emotional-wisdom.

necessity of gratifying the self. And we have all ended up so convinced by the marketing that we no more question the benefit of having strong feelings than at one time we questioned the idea that a sugary, fatty chocolate bar could help us to work, rest and play.

The real trouble with feelings is that they involve a whole lot of things, such as instant sensations, sweet emotionalism, hot stimuli and self, self, self, that have essentially been mis-sold to us as bringers of wellbeing and happiness, while all along being potential causes of brain imbalance and disrupted functioning.

It's enough for now to say that we're all being convinced, by advertising of various forms and for various ends,[4] that feelings are more important than reason when it comes to matters of taste, careers, politics, relationships, business – you name it. And the conviction comes with mental health consequences.

Hotheads in hot hatches are controlling the traffic flow, and pile-ups are happening in our brains. They need more management by the cool classical one before our mental health can get back on track.

---

4   And this includes marketing by stealth, such as in films, books and other art forms, in which the amygdala-driven hot impulses are always more interesting, authentic, sexy and generally desirable than cool, classical reasoning. It hasn't always been this way and it is different in other cultures.

Chapter 5

A balancing (of emotions) act

In the introduction to this book I made a list of some of the main things that I believe are sources of modern mental distress. Most of the items – but especially stress, anxiety and depression – are directly linked to the hyper-tuning of that hot hatch, the amygdala. Too much attention is channelled away from the rest of the brain's 'community needs' by the roar and commotion made by the thoughtless amygdala.

Roar and commotion can sometimes be experienced as pleasurable; in the same way that a fairground ride might be (or even a Teflon-coated sledge) – a sort of emotionally exhilarating but sickly sensation (that sugary image again). It's a feeling that some thrill seekers come to love, but the flipside of excitement can be a kind of urgent, ever-present distress for people who don't 'do' hyper-stimulation. For them, a very similar set of physical symptoms to those of excitement (quickened pulse, changed breathing, tightening in the stomach, etc.) will be experienced as stress or anxiety. Depression operates rather differently, often feeling more like a loss of sensation – but, perhaps, counter-intuitively it also involves heightened activity in the amygdala.

It seems that if we want to tackle stress, anxiety and depression, a good place to start is the amygdala; rather like an over-excitable child, it needs to be calmed down. And, as we've already seen, the best way to suppress all of its noisy anger, fear and anguish is to get the prefrontal cortex to exert its authority and clamp down on the amygdala's feverish activity.

But how is that achieved in real time in the real world? What does the cool classical one have to do to impress its authority on the amygdala? Happily, there are some very practical things we can all do in our everyday behaviour to get this result – and, even more happily, by doing so we can also play a major part in improving the mental health of our own and of future generations.

It may come as something of a shock – given what we're so used to hearing and reading about mental health – to discover what genuinely works to get the better of stress, anxiety and the rest. The following suggestions may appear to be the exact opposite of what we may have been led to believe *should* work,[1] but this is how it really is: we can encourage our prefrontal cortices to squash the exuberance of our amygdalae by *suppressing our emotions, rethinking bad times and events, choosing our words carefully* and *doing something pretty taxing.*

Surprised? Despite the cultural determination to believe that enormous benefits will come from doing more or less the opposite, there is good evidence for all of these suggestions. By challenging the perception that our 'natural' feelings and emotions are somehow honest, authentic and reliable guides for our reactions and behaviour, and by replacing this with the understanding that they are simply physiological sensations which we can interpret and control in a number of ways, we can achieve what we're after – better mental health outcomes – as various studies show.

One such study, carried out at the University of Illinois in 2018, showed that when people were explicitly told to suppress their negative feelings while looking at negative images, there was a reduction of activity in the amygdala and a corresponding reduction in negativity of response, both to 'bad' images and to memories of 'bad' images.[2] This strongly implies that we have the ability to overcome any supposedly natural inclination to wallow in negativity; and negativity, as we already know, is a marker for many mental health conditions. However, as the ability to use that control suggests there is some prefrontal strength already in place, this is possibly better advice for the prevention of depressive and anxious states rather than for the treatment of them.

Perhaps of greater help in that respect is some research from 2014 which showed that if instead of dwelling on the nasty emotional impact of negative personal experiences, we focus on the *context* – the surrounding events, the other people involved, the weather, the clothes we wore and so on – then our negative emotions will dwindle rapidly and the event will be either remembered less or

---

1   Which is often sweeter to our mental taste buds than this slightly tarter and more pragmatic advice will be.

2   Yuta Katsumi and Sandra Dolcos, Suppress to feel and remember less: neural correlates of explicit and implicit emotional suppression on perception and memory, *Neuropsychologia* (2018). DOI: 10.1016/j.neuropsychologia.2018.02.010.

remembered in a less negative light.[3] The researchers found that brain regions involved in basic emotion processing (the amygdala being the most important) were working in conjunction with emotion control regions (the prefrontal cortex) to reduce the emotional impact of memories. They also suggested that simple suppression may not work as well as this more contextualised approach, but one of the researchers was involved in both of these studies and the suppression finding is the more recent of the two.

So, take your pick, but it really does seem that there is a strong association between allowing ourselves full immersion in negative emotions and mental health disorders, and an equally strong one between seeing the bigger picture – looking around and outside yourself – and more positive long-term memories (i.e. better mental health). Knowing what our feelings are in the first place *is* important, if only so that we know when we should be challenging any unhelpful negativity. Once we have recognised our feelings, the best way to alleviate negativity is to contextualise and distance these feelings from the raw emotions.

Other studies using brain imaging have shown that there is a great benefit, in terms of managing disturbing emotions around bad times and events, in being able to reappraise, reframe or rethink highly negative scenes in unemotional terms; that is, there is more upside to being rationally dull in response to them, in refusing to see them in a heightened and emotionally charged light, than there is in bathing ourselves in the sweetness of sorrow or beating ourselves up over our own shortcomings. Reflecting more pragmatically on a bad event reduces activity in the good ole amygdala (surprise, surprise) and increases activity in the good ole – well, guess what!

These and other studies consistently suggest that amygdala behaviour has to be *actively* squashed (I prefer that to quashed – it's more graphic) by prefrontal activity. This very conscious approach to changing thought patterns is what you should get with CBT therapy,

---

3   Ekaterina Denkova, Sandra Dolcos and Florin Dolcos, Neural correlates of 'distracting' from emotion during autobiographical recollection, *Social Cognitive and Affective Neuroscience* 10(2) (2015): 219–230.

if it is well carried out.[4] As Shakespeare has already told us, it's really a case of, 'there is nothing either good or bad, but thinking makes it so'.[5]

This neatly brings us on to the next bit of armour we can use to defend against mental health problems – language – because how else do we think except in language? So, other than making other things good or bad, what is language good for? As I will be saying quite a bit more about language in the next chapter, for now I will stick to its usefulness in regulating emotion. There will be some overlap with things I discuss later on, so just bear with me. Because, let's face it, language is the massively complex development that makes us human, and if I understood and could communicate all its secrets I would be in charge of something like a Max Planck Institute, with little time for writing a book like this!

In linguistics there is a proposal called the 'Sapir–Whorf hypothesis', which in a rather sideways fashion brought academics' attention to the question of whether language is an outcome of thought or actually determines, or makes, meaning and therefore leads to thoughts. As this book is not an academic treatise I will leave the academics there and simply state that the debate about what language is and what it does carries on, but that most experts agree that language, in both cultures and individuals, appears to do double duty, *affecting* and *reflecting* their ideas and their emotions. Brain imaging studies show strong two-way links between the language and emotion centres of the brain, as well as between the language centres and more reflective regions.

It is conceivable that language may go back much further than previously thought – in fact, as far back as 400,000 years. If so, it is likely to have first developed as a tool for communication between early forms of humanity who were struggling for survival in a hostile environment, rather than as a form of personal emotional processing. However, according to anthropologist Jerome Lewis of University College London, one thing language did eventually

---

4   What might be called 'semi-spiritual' approaches like mindfulness and meditation are often held up as working equally well to alleviate depression, but although they can be useful there is little solid evidence for them being universal solutions. In fact, there is evidence that they can result in psychosis in vulnerable people. See Miguel Farias and Catherine Wikholm, *The Buddha Pill: Can Meditation Change You?* (London: Watkins Publishing, 2015); Duncan Barford, Dark night of the soul, *Therapy Today* 29(6) (2018): 34–37; and Barbara Ehrenreich, *Natural Causes: Life, Death and the Illusion of Control* (London: Granta, 2018).

5   *Hamlet*, II, ii.

achieve was the creation of a shared human identity, with its suggestion of an 'us'.[6] That sense of being plural, of needing to cooperate, must have been really important for survival, because 'us' would so obviously work better than 'I' when it came to hunting, caring for young and so on. It also makes sense that as long as 'we' was more important than 'me', then originally my sensations were not going to have too many words attached to them.

But that, of course, was then. Over time certain individual physical sensations did come to have words attached to them, and clearly the most intense sensations were likely to have been the cause of some of the earliest words for what we call emotions. However, intense sensations are very easily confused. How do you sense elation? Or fear? They are really quite similar at a physiological level, and that is where the affecting/reflecting business comes in. If we've been taught to call a sensation 'elation', then we are likely to see it as positive and regard ourselves as happy, which will generate brain chemicals that are positive and motivating. A mental win-win. If, on the other hand, we have been taught to call an identical sensation 'fear' (the same can be said for the dual terms of surprise and fear), the ensuing brain chemicals and brain activity will be very different and the outcome is more likely to be negativity and depression. A mental lose-lose.

In the United States a schools programme called Ruler, developed by the Yale Center for Emotional Intelligence, has used this principle to teach schoolchildren to interpret physiological changes in their bodies linked to emotions, label them in an appropriately healthy way and then learn strategies to regulate those emotions more effectively.[7] It has apparently been very successful, even resulting in improved relationships between students and teachers. All of which rather goes to prove that emotions do not have to be the drivers of behaviour, and that with a re-engineering of the language used about them we can massively impact their effect on us. Which is definitely the case when we're talking about that relationship between 'I' and the world beyond.

Another language-based technique comes out of studies showing that more resilient people often use the word 'you' rather than 'I' to help them cope with negative experiences. This works for the benefit of mental health because it depersonalises what may have

---

6   David Robson, Finding our voice, *New Scientist* 242(3228) (2019): 34–37.
7   See www.rulerapproach.org.

been an unpleasant personal experience, making it more universal, more distant, less pointed and less threatening or victimising. If 'it could happen to anyone', then it is a useful life lesson – it is 'meaning making' in the jargon.[8] It adds to rather than detracts from experience. Using 'you' rather than 'I', of course, also limits any tendency to ruminate, dwell or generally fixate on those personal (amygdala-biased) emotions.

Basically, it seems as if the emotionally constipated and distancing linguistic habits of the early to mid-twentieth century, which were so easily mocked by the emotionally literate of the 1960s onwards, turn out to be psychologically healthier much of the time.[9] Who knew!

If you can distance yourself even further from yourself, it turns out to be even better again, because talking to yourself in the third person (remember your grammar homework?) can actually help you to control your emotions. A study carried out by researchers at Michigan State University indicated that the psychological distance created by referring to yourself as a third party (said Gillian, as she reflected on how this approach was helping her to deal with the time pressure of getting this book out) can be helpful for emotional regulation and self-control, and can even be seen in reduced activity in relevant areas of the brain (and we know what we're talking about there, don't we?).[10] Of course, it helps if you keep the conversation on the silent side, otherwise your amazingly good mental health may not always be acknowledged and appreciated by those around you.

I've also suggested this technique to clients who are trying to quit smoking or challenge some other hot stimulus, and it's worked remarkably well. 'Hey, why is Stanley going back to the old ways

---

8   Making sense out of life events, giving them a shape and purpose so we do not feel at the mercy of disorder or pointlessness.

9   Linguistic distancing can help to regulate emotions for people with autism spectrum conditions. They process experiences differently in the first place, and forcing them to talk about their feelings or to 'own them' (i.e. speak about them in the first person) can result in them making something up to please a therapist or counsellor, which may be experienced as coercive and bullying. Much harm has unintentionally been caused in this way.

10 Jason Moser, Adrienne Dougherty, Whitney Mattson, Benjamin Katz, Tim Moran, Darwin Guevarra, Holly Shablack, Ozlem Ayduk, John Jonides, Marc Berman and Ethan Kross, Third person self-talk facilitates emotion regulation without engaging cognitive control: converging evidence from ERP and fMRI, *Scientific Reports* 7 (2017), article 4519. DOI: 10.1038/s41598-017-04047-3.

that only make him feel crap? What's he thinking of, spending a tenner on fags, when he needs that money to buy his mum a birthday present?' It all helps to keep that rampant beast of an amygdala at a distance and in its place.

The other, perhaps highly counter-intuitive, strategy for dealing with emotional overload that I mentioned near the start of this chapter was 'doing something pretty taxing'. This notion must be about as challenging to some models of mental health care as could be. But I can vouch for its effectiveness from my own personal experience, because when I suffered a totally unexpected and potentially overwhelmingly emotional family bereavement, I also had a work-related deadline to meet, one which left very little wriggle room and which was going to involve a big cognitive load. In other words, a lot of head work. I can only say thank you to those who needed that work doing to such a tight schedule. It kept me functioning at a very difficult time, and helped to ease my passage into healthful mourning and sadness, bypassing any possibility of all-enveloping destructive grief.

It turns out that I might not be the only person who has been helped by having to think quite hard when emotions start to flood. The cognitive load is a form of bulwark against a sea of troubles and a flood of emotions. Indeed, a study carried out a few years ago showed that after exposure to negative images, which inevitably stirred the amygdala into action, a short sharp dose of demanding maths raised activity levels in the prefrontal cortex and so tuned them down in the amygdala.[11] That may sound relatively trivial, but just multiply the effect and the sum total is better mental health.

It's not a particularly surprising outcome once we start to understand how the brain works. So, how is it that so many people with professional status and/or other forms of influence seem not to 'get it' at all? Far too often, going home and resting is still the given prescription for emotional upset (as it has been for many physical problems, such as backache, although it's now realised that rest is the worst solution in most cases and controlled exercise the best). You might as well be told to take time out to ruminate, fixate on yourself and your emotions, give your amygdala free rein – and feel considerably worse. A big brain workout, like a physical workout,

11 Lotte Van Dillen, Dirk Heslenfeld and Sander Koole, Tuning down the emotional brain: an fMRI study of the effects of cognitive load on the processing of affective images, *Neuroimage* 45(4) (2009): 1212–1219.

will leave you tired, and that at least will leave less mental space for negativity and depression to colonise.

The conclusion is that emotion, like sugar, is best taken in small doses if we care about our health.

Parents' takeaway for balancing emotion

The first suggestion here is actually a 'would-be parents' takeaway, because parenting for good mental health is now known to start long before conception! Up to two-thirds of young pregnant women in London have a mental health problem, often depression and anxiety,[12] and as it is well understood that depression in pregnancy increases the likelihood of mental and behavioural problems in the children of those women, it is clear that something must be done. Recent work in epigenetics[13] suggests that we should be doing more to help young women with their own mental health problems so that we can help their children in turn, so this advice is for both parents and their kids.

- Think beautiful thoughts. Like many young mothers, I used to laugh at the advice from previous generations, especially suggestions like this which seemed mimsy and patronising to a feisty young feminist, but it turns out to have been good advice after all. And, no, it's not easy when your job is hard (or non-existent), when you're struggling to make ends meet and maybe you're even struggling to get pregnant in the first place, but faking it to make it is definitely a winner on this one. If you can turn your thoughts towards the positives in your life and suppress all those negative ones (do like the marshmallow kids – distract yourself until the second one pops up), not only will

---

12 Georgia Lockwood Estrin, Elizabeth G. Ryan, Kylee Trevillion and Jill Demilew, Young pregnant women and risk for mental disorders: findings from an early pregnancy cohort, *British Journal of Psychiatry Open* 5(2) (2019): e21. DOI: https://doi.org/10.1192/bjo.2019.6.

13 Epigenetics is the study of how heritable changes in the way genes (either active or inactive) are expressed can lead to changes in the way our cells work, without in any way altering our underlying DNA. Bodies and brains can 'inherit' things like anxiety, depression, hyperactivity, obesity and heart disease as a result of parental and even grandparental behaviour and experiences. This is a newish field of scientific research and much is still to be discovered, but it seems clear that what we eat and drink and how we behave can influence the future of generations to come.

you eventually train yourself to do it more easily and kick-start all the hormones that will reward you and your (future) baby with calmer moods, but you will also save yourself from the often thanklessly hard task of bringing up an anxious or hyperactive child.[14]

Being highly excitable and full-on can make it feel like you're having the time of your life (and, boy, is the infantilising approach of advertisers to be blamed for the perception that even adults can live like they are in an endless playtime – what fun all the vibrant colours and jolly shouty behaviour!), but parenting asks everyone to grow up a bit. Carrying on with a hyper lifestyle (I'll describe some of the things that go with that later) may lead to churned up hormones and an ever revved up amygdala. Again, even before pregnancy a woman should think about toning down some of the excitability. This could mean driving in a way that avoids inciting road rage in yourself and others, or engaging in measured debate and assertive behaviour rather than in furious rows and soap-inspired melodramatics. We seem to be culturally confused about the meaning of excitability, too often assuming that it's the same thing as happiness. People who are full on, apparently 24/7, are only too often the same people who behind the scenes are down as much as up. How many times after a suicide do we read that it came as a surprise to everyone, as he/she was always 'the life and soul of the party'? Better for us all if we accept that balanced emotions are better for mental wellness than excessive emotions, and aim to achieve just that.

It's not all down to mothers. Men pass on epigenetic changes, too. Much of this advice applies to both sexes, and even when it doesn't it is still everyone's responsibility to create an environment that will work best for our mental health, so we could all tone things down for the sake of future generations. Shouting, screaming and acting in unrestrained ways in public places, whether by children or adults who should know better, is (a) experienced by many people as aggressive and/or alarming, and (b) is showing anyone with an ounce of knowledge that those doing it are not so much in the grip of pleasure as being dragged along in the wake of the amygdala. All children

14 Claire Hughes, Rory Devine, Judi Mesman and Clancy Blair, Parental wellbeing, couple relationship quality and children's behavior problems in the first two years of life, *Development & Psychopathology* 8 (2019): 597–600.

scream from time to time, nothing to worry about there, but when you can hear one voice above all the others in a playground which carries on ramping up the excitement for longer, then you might reasonably start to worry about the child's future wellbeing. The same applies to groups of teens or adults 'having fun' on a Friday or Saturday night.

- When it comes to dealing with children's bad experiences or behaviour – and all your best efforts won't result in an eternally calm and easy child (hopefully!) – as with yourself, the most effective approach involves damping down the effect of any nasty emotional experiences by focusing on the context, the surrounding events, the people involved, the weather, the clothes and so on. Talk about these elements and ask the child to think about them and describe them, rather than simply dwelling on their own negative feelings. Primarily you want to take their mind elsewhere. This works surprisingly well for problems like fear of flying, too (for those of any age). If fear takes hold, but preferably before it does, ask the child (or adult) to think about a place like their bedroom or the contents of their wardrobe, and then get them to work slowly and methodically around the space, describing how it all fits together, or giving detail about colours, textures and so on. All that hard thinking helps to tone down all that hard emoting.

- There is also normalising – generalising an experience to help children see that there is some social meaning to what has happened or has been experienced – which is where the reframing or re-engineering of language comes in. If your child hears you say to yourself over some disappointment or other, 'Oh well, you can't always have what you want – if you did, the world would soon run out of chocolate,' they learn both how to keep strong emotion under the thumb of the prefrontal cortex and that there is a reason for the things that happen, a sense to life (which is always comforting). Similarly with self-motivational mutterings like, 'Mummy is feeling a bit cross; people often do when they're trying to fit too much in. She will feel a whole lot better if she just sits down for a minute and makes herself a to-do list.' There is a recognition of the strong emotion, but it is coupled with a regulating thought and connected by third-person phrasing to a generalisation. It goes from being a potential (and anxiety-provoking) shouty thing to being a useful life lesson model in how to balance emotion with reason.

- Doing something pretty taxing doesn't have to mean giving your children frequent tests in advanced mathematics, but it might involve expecting them to carry on with schoolwork if they have suffered bereavement or some other crisis. Over many years in education, I did not notice that young people who were given time off or extra time in exams for psychiatric reasons were any the better for the approach taken. It tended to validate their 'difference'. I worked with many students who were allowed to take exams separately because of various physical disabilities, including extreme visual handicap, and was usually blown away by how little extra consideration they thought necessary once the practicalities had been sorted out. The challenges they faced on a regular basis made them tough cookies. Anxiety and depression are real – I'm not suggesting they are imagined – but giving the expression of them free rein, by allowing them to dictate how a young person's life is lived, is often a way to validate that young person's loss of autonomy to the amygdala and to reinforce their helplessness. Parents can help here by gradually building up their child's confidence in their ability to cope before exam time or new experiences (such as university) with small incremental challenges in daily life and with physically taxing exercise that will help to both tone down the emotion and create a template for mentally taxing exercise. Learning that immersion in something that needs full concentration is one of the best ways to knock out worry and anxiety is one of the greatest life lessons a parent can give.

- Lastly, modelling desirable behaviour. This will come up everywhere because it's one of the most important things any of us can do to help beat mental distress. It's no good saying to anyone, let alone a child or young person, 'Calm down, you're way too excited!' or 'How can you overreact in that way? It's just not important,' if you usually shout at every other driver on the road or go ape when you're thwarted in some way. Calm and balanced is as calm and balanced does, and children are usually highly attuned to hypocrisy.

Educators' takeaway for balancing emotion

Although people involved in the earlier phases of education (and anyone involved in providing emotional support services) are not in the same situation as parents in being able to affect outcomes long before a child is even a twinkle in their eye, they can still do a fair amount before a child is involved in very formal education. As we've seen in the marshmallow work, small children can be proficient in advanced mental processes such as delaying gratification, which means that they can control their amygdalae with their prefrontal cortices – that is, balance their emotions.

If they can't do this, then they also won't be much good at queuing, waiting patiently or turn taking in class. Not only might this lead to them being unpopular in school, but they are also going to be more at risk of developing mental health problems and of having a shorter lifespan. This may sound like rather too huge a claim, until we look at the statistics. Poor self-control and patience result in poorer literacy, as children just don't have the concentration needed for learning. Low literacy levels are associated with shorter life expectancy – up to 26 years shorter for a boy in a high-risk area, according to findings from the National Literacy Trust.[15] That is a good enough reason to start rectifying any self-control issues the moment a child comes into the system, so here are some ideas to help achieve that.

- Rather than the theoretically beneficial more, use fewer pictures and less colour and informality in the classroom. I'm not advocating a pared down monastic atmosphere, but the evidence is that too much stimulation can be confusing and arousing; the ideal for learning is calm and order. This is especially true for children who may have chaotic home lives and little experience of routine.[16] Recent research from the University of Sussex has even shown that illustrations need to be used sparingly in early years education, as having more than one per page is so confusing that it hampers the child's ability to follow text – even though they may not yet be able to read. Single-picture pages resulted in twice as much word learning as

---

15 National Literacy Trust, Life expectancy shortened by 26 years for children growing up in areas with the most serious literacy problems (15 February 2018) [press release]. Available at: https://literacytrust.org.uk/news/life-expectancy-shortened-26-years-children-growing-areas-most-serious-literacy-problems.

16 Half the 'bad boys' I have ever taught wanted to join the army. It was as though they yearned for certainty and discipline, without having the first idea of how to create it for themselves.

two-picture pages.[17] It really is a case of less is more when it comes to stimulation and learning-ready brains.

- The same principle applies to content. Even books for very young children often have an agenda and may pitch things in rather emotive language. Words like 'sad' and 'lonely' appear quite frequently, often because it is assumed that children need to have their experiences validated and affirmed in an empathetic attempt to engage with them. This is a noble concept but it is flawed. In the early stages of education children are learning how to interpret both the world and their own sensations, and if these are expressed in negative ways too routinely then something like sadness, even depression, will become a given in their lives. So less is most definitely more when it comes to emotional literacy at such young ages. Helping children to develop more rational and less emotional responses to experiences will improve their emotional wellbeing.[18]

- In the same vein, but for older pupils and students, it has long been taken as given that teaching creative subjects and taking creative courses out of or after school are totally on the side of the mental health angels. Sadly – and I speak as a sometime teacher and lecturer in English – it's just not that straightforward. It all depends on *how* the subjects are taught.

- It's known that poets are at greater than average risk of depression, and there is evidence that suicidal poets who eventually die by suicide use more first-person pronouns ('I') than those who do not in the end kill themselves, and both use more first-person pronouns than non-suicidal poets.[19] Not a cheery subject, but helpful in that it tells us that creativity which comes in the form of self-expression may in fact be rather bad for us. The least worst interpretation is that depressed people

17 Zoe M. Flack and Jessica S. Horst, Two sides to every story: children learn words better from one storybook page at a time, *Infant and Child Development* 27(1) (2018): e2047.

18 Contrary to many popular beliefs about the brain, what we have learned from brain damage cases is that the left side of the brain, the rational side (although it's not quite as simple as that), is much more positive and optimistic than the right so-called creative and emotional side. Poetry, especially when it doesn't follow 'rules', and is grammatically and linguistically free-form, is more likely to depend on the right-hand depressive side of the brain. Given any inherent teenage negativity, writing in this way is likely to make depression worse.

19 Shannon W. Stirman and James W. Pennebaker, Word use in the poetry of suicidal and nonsuicidal poets, *Psychosomatic Medicine* 63(4) (2001): 517–522.

turn to poetry, but if that is the case it doesn't seem as if poetry is helping them much. They might find it more helpful if they wrote about subjects other than themselves and in more objective language, but then Tennyson did quite a bit of that and remained stubbornly depressive for most of his life.[20] Another solution could be to put experiences into a more positive, rational framework or to tell stories in a more light-hearted way. But Wendy Cope does that and Dorothy Parker is humour personified, and both are still essentially depressive. Perhaps it's poetry itself that is the problem, and so if creativity is to be expressed in words it should be in the form of prose. Practising writing in more structured, orderly (pro-prefrontal) ways, including argument and counter-argument as well as personal opinion, may well be best for mental health.

- Other creative subjects have been found to be associated with negativity, depression and sadness, too.[21] According to a study carried out by psychologists, teens who took part in activities such as music, drama and painting were more likely to say they were sad or depressed. Although it wasn't clear if it was a case of chicken or egg, the researchers realised that lack of involvement in health-promoting sports could not be to blame, as there was no difference between teens who took part in both and those who only did creative activities. They concluded that the association was a simple one: teen depression and 'arty' activities were linked, one way or another, but possibly because arts activities can be solo and introverted, and there is a strong link between introversion (otherwise known as self-absorption) and depression.

- Whatever advocates say, there is absolutely no proven relationship between studying and practising arts subjects and better mental health – and the opposite might even apply. Although undergraduate and postgraduate students across many disciplines appear to have higher than average rates of anxiety, there is some evidence that once students move on into their career, those who studied management and engineering

---

20 See Kay Redfield Jamison's *Touched with Fire: Manic-Depressive Illness and the Artistic Temperament* (New York: Free Press, 1993) for an interesting perspective on creativity and mental health.

21 Laura Young, Ellen Winner and Sara Cordes, Heightened incidence of depressive symptoms in adolescents involved in the arts, *Psychology of Aesthetics, Creativity, and the Arts* 7(2) (2013): 197–202.

will have better long-term wellbeing than those who studied arts-based subjects. None of this is much more than anecdotal, but it tends to suggest that more pragmatic or practical studies might be more 'brain healthy' than the ones that usually get promoted as such – if only because they will be inevitably less emotionally stirring (less of that hyper amygdala activity) and also taught in a more measured way.[22]

This brings me to what might be called 'The Passion of Miss Jean Brodie' or of many other teachers who see their role as being to inspire their young charges – but sadly not always entirely for their subject, so much as for the sake of the sweet feeling itself. I am in a very passionate relationship myself – with William Shakespeare – and so I have no wish to make studying a subject dry, dusty or fusty. I also believe (unless hundreds of students have been lying) that I have done a pretty good job of enthusing them about their studies and about literature. And I hope I have encouraged them to be analytical, open-minded and discriminating (I refuse to see that as a dirty word). I have, though, worked alongside many teachers and lecturers who appeared to be keener to whip up students' passions for 'causes' – even wearing T-shirts covered in less than educational slogans. Perhaps they should remember that Othello says, 'it is the cause, my soul',[23] to justify the fact that he is about to suffocate his innocent wife (there isn't much that Shakespeare doesn't cover somewhere in his work)! But passion for causes isn't only harmful when it makes someone overlook rational evidence to justify their irrational acts; taken to obsessive extremes it is yet another way that the self-generated pleasure chemicals associated with rectitude (a largely inflexible, narrow perspective on a matter) can feel a whole lot sweeter than a chocolate biscuit.

Passion shouldn't be confused with knowledge, and it shouldn't prevent a teacher from putting across alternative viewpoints to their students. Jean Brodie, with her passionate but narrow

---

22 Learning practical, hands-on and often repetitive skills which promote hand–eye coordination and a more tactile learning experience appear to work well to calm anxiety. The National Trust is even supporting 'caveman therapy' courses which help men to learn bushcraft and survival skills and seem to work as an antidote to anxiety. If nothing else, it is doing something pretty taxing at the physical level. See Jordan Dunbar, Cavemen therapy: can being a caveman cure anxiety?, *BBC News* (3 August 2019) [video]. Available at: https://www.bbc.co.uk/news/av/health-49211802/cavemen-therapy-can-being-a-caveman-cure-anxiety.

23 *Othello*, V, ii.

mindset, caused a lot of harm to her girls. She would have done them much more good had she helped them to understand the importance of balance, rather than passion, in terms of feelings, and helped them to keep theirs more under wraps, look at ideas from a number of different perspectives, and talk less about personal opinions and more about what objective material they could bring to bear on them. Simply thinking that it's enough to be passionate about something for it to be both true and unassailable is a royal high road to anxiety and mental distress. Passions have an awful tendency to be inflexible and all about me and my amygdala. Teaching, when it works for the mental health of future generations, should not be about gratifying teachers' own existing emotional needs (however sweet that may feel); done well, it should develop perspectives and perceptions on both sides and so help both teachers and students to grow emotionally.

● When it comes to 'doing something pretty taxing', there has been a relentless campaign by some commentators and theorists to limit students' exposure to anything much beyond 'doing something that feels copable with'. This has not been a good development for mental health, as it affirms any pre-existing belief that life should be easy and comfortable, when that is patently impossible to achieve for seven billion of us. And there is evidence to suggest that long hours and frequent testing are not the problems that critics seem to want them to be. In 2017, the Organisation for Economic Co-operation and Development (an intergovernmental organisation with thirty-six member countries) found there was no link between long hours of study and students' sense of satisfaction. They also found that frequency of tests was unrelated to anxiety about school. However, they did find that relationships between students, teachers and parents did affect how they felt, and that supportive, responsive and helpful teachers made for motivated and better performing students.[24]

Young people can take a lot, when the right backing is in place, and that includes dealing with a lot emotionally at challenging times, so perhaps we should be rethinking how we deal with

---

24 Andreas Schleicher, Parents make a big difference just by talking, *BBC News* (19 April 2017). Available at: www.bbc.co.uk/news/business-39577514.

times of crisis.[25] Again, it has become a given in some minds that rest and time away from studies is the solution to tragic events, but research has shown that suppressing our emotions, at least as a first resort in a crisis, not only helps people to get necessary practical things done, but it also allows bodily responses to settle and normalise. There are such strong connections between the amygdala, the hippocampus and prefrontal brain regions that by creating order with the influence of prefrontal cortex (however chaotic things are), we inevitably damp down the hot amygdala, which in turn affects how memories get laid down, making them potentially less emotionally impactful, if not less unpleasant as such. To help youngsters deal with difficult times in life, it looks as if it is better to offer as much understanding, help and support as possible, while still expecting them to turn up to classes, put in the hours and perform reasonably well academically. This will help to normalise normal, and will help them to cope better with potentially overwhelming emotions, as well as leaving them at a reduced risk of re-traumatising recall.

- Modelling desirable behaviour applies just as much to anyone charged with educating our children and adolescents as it does to parents. I will never forget going to an end-of-term school assembly which had been run (very sweetly and effectively) by junior school pupils, which had left parents and grandparents moved and thoughtful. The moment of calm was completely shattered by the new young head teacher running down the central aisle, arms waving and loudly trilling, 'Kids, you were *awesome*, simply awesome. Parents, grans and granddads, you were *awesome*, simply awesome.' Such hyper-excitability and unimaginative language from on high didn't suggest that she understood children's developmental needs quite as well as she thought she did. There are enough children with attention deficit hyperactivity disorder (ADHD) already. Emotionally controlled and soothing adults aren't experienced as boring or colourless; they are much more likely to be experienced as engaged, responsive and available. Much more emotionally in tune, in fact.

---

25 Shakespeare and his peers would have been at school from daybreak to nightfall, and there is nothing I know of to suggest that they suffered from mental exhaustion. Mostly they went on to cope with phenomenal workloads as a matter of course – although he did write a good lunatic.

We should be looking at helping youngsters to manage their emotions better, rather than immerse themselves in their emotions. If I'm right, then encouraging immersion in personal feelings has at least been partly responsible for the mental distress that so many are self-declaring they are experiencing at the moment. Earlier in this chapter we considered the (huge) question of whether meaning is made by language, or vice versa, and questioned whether feelings are 'real' or whether they may in fact be interpretations of sensations which are made good or bad through specific cultural uses of language. In the next chapter, we're going to take a further look at some of these possibilities and also at other ways in which language may make or break our emotional selves.

Chapter 6

Language matters

Language matters because essentially it is what makes us human; it allows us to think consciously and to communicate at a distance. Therefore, it stands to reason that there must be all kinds of complexity attached to the brain systems that create language, as well as to the ways in which we use it.

As with other complex brain systems, language turns out to be of vital importance to mental health and to social skills, in themselves associated with both mental wellbeing and long-term protection against dementia.[1] In December 2016, the *Sunday Times* reported that schools were having to employ speech therapists for 3-year-olds because so many of them had such poor language abilities that they were using pushing and shoving to communicate; apparently they couldn't even understand 'positional instructions' such as 'stand behind', as they didn't have the necessary vocabulary. Julie Lachkovic, a lecturer overseeing the project, described the problem as very worrying and said the aim was to teach children how to use language to 'form and stay in relationships; to play games; to use language to pretend and to … find out about the world'.[2] In other words (and that phrase in itself is an indication of how language gives us flexibility of thought as well as choices about actions), to teach children how to be fully human.

Having a narrow vocabulary inevitably impacts on school grades, but it also results in impoverishment of broader human objectives, behaviours and relationships, because how else do we understand or express any of those things except through language? The more complex and sophisticated the language, the more complex and sophisticated everything else can be.

---

1 This begins at the earliest ages because cognitive reserve – which is the result of good, lifelong education and the laying down of both information and strong neural networks so that information can be deployed in complex ways – is one of the strongest defences we have against a decline in brain function.

2 Nicholas Hellen, Speech therapy for 3-year-olds who shove to make friends, *Sunday Times* (4 December 2016).

But language isn't simply vocabulary; we may know lots of words – even birds can manage that much – but who wants to be a bird-brain? (And, yes, I know birds are being shown to have amazing abilities, but still!) And there are types and types of words. Some are simply names for things, and these are associated with parts of the brain that do what is called declarative or explicit memory (basically recalling information) – very useful, if not essential, for some aspects of life, but not particularly sophisticated when it comes to under-standing people and relationships; these need something more.[3] Grammar can be very helpful for many processes, including linking thoughts together (more on this later), but it uses similar brain cir-cuits to what is called procedural memory, which involves remembering sequences (just as grammar does) that are needed to do things that require chains of actions, like riding a bike or playing a musical instrument. Again, jolly useful, but not totally linked to working out people.

That is where function words come in. A US academic called James Pennebaker is a supreme master when it comes to these, having researched them endlessly. Function words include pronouns, articles, prepositions, conjunctions, auxiliary verbs, negatives and many common adverbs (Google these terms now if you need to!). Pennebaker asserts that function words are processed differently in the brain and that we need social skills to understand them and use them. He has done in-depth studies using the latest computerised text analysis methods, and concludes that function words are more reliable indicators of psychological states than other words. For example, pronoun use can indicate an inward-looking or outward-looking state of mind, and preposition and conjunction use are associated with complexity of thought (it's a pity that continuity announcers seem to have lost this skill). He suggests that close computer analysis of function word use can reveal more about a student's potential success than any human judge ever could, because it can get into the depths of *how* a person thinks, rather than *what* they are thinking about.

One outcome of his work has been to show that higher grades at universities in the United States are achieved with greater article

---

3   Including understanding yourself and your own motivations. It is possible that people on the autistic spectrum may have overly developed capacity in a declarative way, being good at facts and detail, but may have underdeveloped areas of the brain that in other people connect information and emotion and which for them create complex relationships in both the social and cognitive spheres.

and preposition use, which indicate recognition of complexly organised objects and concepts, while lower grades are associated with more personal narratives, using greater numbers of auxiliaries, pronouns, adverbs and conjunctions.[4] It's impossible for me to say if the same is true in the UK, but there is likely to be a correlation between more personal, inward-looking narratives and less robust mental health.

Here is Pennebaker again: 'Depressed people use the word "I" much more often than emotionally stable people.' The more people switched from using first-person singular pronouns (I, me, my) to other pronouns (we, you, she, they) from one piece of writing to the next, the better their health became. Their word use reflected their psychological state. And it's not even that there is necessarily an association between 'I' and dark and depressive language in general, because by analysing poems by writers who died by suicide and those who didn't, he found not the dark content he had expected to find but 'significant differences in the frequency of words like "I". In study after study, we kept finding the same thing.'[5]

Other research has thrown up similar or related findings, recognising that as people develop greater maturity and sense of social responsibility, self-centred language decreases and complexity and nuance in language grows. This means using words that imply more than one simple or fixed set of possibilities; words such as 'but' or 'although' carry these possibilities, and there are many others – in fact, 'or' is one. Anything which allows that life is made up of lots of possibly competing considerations indicates complex thinking,

---

4   Narrative writing is a different kettle of fish when it is telling broader stories – ones that entertain others. Stories that involve society, other people, outside events, the past and so on often come from writers with good social skills and a wide circle of friends, both of which are associated with relatively good mental health.

    In some prisons there has been a push to get inmates writing personal narratives to help them become more emotionally articulate and to encourage (supposedly) healthful creativity. I have come across teachers whose good intentions are not matched by their psychological understanding, who have left quite disturbed prisoners to 'express themselves' for hours at a time. Not only have these inarticulate first-person ramblings done little for their learning, but their already wayward thought processes have become even more entrenched. Such initiatives, which have some merit when done well, need to be carried out only by very well-qualified people. It's not good enough to *feel* good about doing this kind of thing. We must *know* that the process works.

5   James W. Pennebaker, Your use of pronouns reveals your personality, *Harvard Business Review* (December 2011). Available at: https://hbr.org/2011/12/your-use-of-pronouns-reveals-your-personality.

especially when it moves the debate from the personal to a broader level. Complex thinking is definitely better for mental health.

This is shown yet again in research from a team at the University of Reading which, like Pennebaker, also used computerised analysis to check huge amounts of text, much of it taken from online forums.[6] The team again looked into the obsession with I, myself and me, also finding that people with depression are focused on themselves and less connected to others, but adding some rather interesting findings about the use of what they term 'absolutist language'. This, in effect, reflects what we call black and white thinking – thinking in which there is none of that flexibility which we now know is better for mental health. Absolutist language might include words like 'never', 'always', 'nothing' and 'completely', as well as phrases that I have heard used very often in therapy: 'no question', 'no doubt', 'no two ways about it'.

What they also found, on looking specifically into depression and suicide-related forums, where the use of absolutist language was anywhere from 50–80% higher than average, was that even when people felt they were recovering, and were using these sites to express optimism (in highly positive language), they were still using more than average numbers of absolutist words, which does not bode well for their long-term prospects.

One thing that *I* can say, with absolute certainty, is that *language matters*. But for too long we seem to have been treating language as a tool to express our selves, our feelings and our opinions, rather than as a way of establishing those selves as connected-up members of a hugely complex society, with lots of competing demands.[7]

---

6   Mohammed Al-Mosaiwi and Tom Johnstone, In an absolute state: elevated use of absolutist words is a marker specific to anxiety, depression, and suicidal ideation, *Clinical Psychological Science* 6(4) (2018): 529–542. Available at: https://journals. sagepub.com/doi/full/10.1177/2167702617747074.

7   Two studies by medical researcher Werdie van Staden (cited in Alan Priest, Let's you and I talk, *Therapy Today* 22(10) (2011): 24–28) which investigated first-person pronoun use by patients showed a distinction between worse outcome cases whose use of 'I' was associated with a sense of incapacity and 'loss of agency' or self-efficacy, and better outcome cases whose use suggested personal agency or responsibility. Patients were no longer positioning themselves as victims. See Werdie van Staden, *Linguistic Changes During Recovery: A Philosophical and Empirical Study of First Person Pronoun Usage and the Semantic Positions of Patients as Expressed in Psychotherapy and Mental Illness*. Unpublished dissertation, University of Warwick (1999); Werdie van Staden, Linguistic markers of recovery: theoretical underpinnings of first person pronoun usage and semantic positions of patients, *Philosophy, Psychiatry and Psychology* 9(2) (2003): 105–121.

Is it possible that some of what we have been promoting as good for us – in parts of westernised society, at least – has been actively encouraging vulnerability to mental health problems? Even if it's not yet clear whether by getting people to change their language use we can help to improve their mental health, it's very likely that steering them away from language that focuses their thoughts inwards, minutely exploring and interpreting their own sensations and emotions, and instead towards language that connects them to the world beyond themselves, creating meaning making for their own experiences at the same time, can only be a good thing. Surely?

Parents' takeaway for boosting pro-mental health language skills

- Talking and reading to children from the earliest age, long before they can obviously understand, is hugely helpful in developing language skills. Help them to appreciate that words are beautiful and living things that will give them endless fun as they get bigger and older. But they don't have to be restricted to 'baby language', even though it does help to keep the tone and register (style and formality) age-appropriate.

- Don't spend very long (if any time at all) on mobile phones when with your children because (a) they dislike it intensely, because you're making them feel unimportant and neglected, and (b) they learn nothing from it. Keep chatting to them and talking about life in general. This will help them to learn about social attitudes and relationships between objects, especially if you use lots of those function words as they are growing up.

- Use agentic language yourself in order to model taking responsibility for behaviour and ideas, rather than constantly talking about personal feelings and opinions. Create a balance between the two.

Here is a story which crosses the boundaries of parenting and education and tells a cautionary tale about parental attitudes to learning and authority, language use and mental wellbeing. I was running a communications course in a women's prison. Most of the women attending were inside for emotionally driven crimes that had hurt them as much as anyone else – for example, setting fire to their own homes. Why? They didn't have the appropriate communication skills to tell the council and other authorities about situations and relationships which were getting out of hand. Instead, they shouted, insulted and, when things got really bad, simply turned to self-sabotaging destruction.

I was helping them to develop more appropriate ways of engaging with formal life in general (more formal than cursing and swearing, anyway), and the course involved telling stories in ways that were likely to get a sympathetic hearing. I suggested to one woman that she could add a few adjectives to her story for colour and interest, and someone questioned, 'What's an adjective?' I asked if they had heard of nouns: 'No.' Verbs: 'No.' I asked if they would like a quick skim through the parts of speech: 'Yes, please.'

Ten minutes later, after a stunned silence, one woman asked on behalf of the group, 'Why has no one told us all this before?'

Those women may well have been exposed to nouns and verbs before, but possibly they had also been emotionally bullied by inadequate parents into believing that school couldn't tell them anything that was worth listening to or that could ever be of value to them. Which was untrue, of course, as those women were very happy to realise. They finally walked away from the course with their language use infinitely improved, certificates in hand, heads held high and futures brighter.

Parents are hugely important in setting up their children for lifelong learning, which can lead to lifelong improvements in mental health, and even to later life protection against losing it.

Educators' takeaway for boosting pro-mental health language skills

- Despite the fact that Shakespeare and other writers from one of the most creative periods in literary history spent long hours during their schooldays learning rules and techniques, mostly in Latin, educational theory in the latter half of the twentieth century held that prescriptive teaching was bad for students' creativity and wellbeing. A number of writers, including James Joyce and Virginia Woolf, recognised for their more experimental writing, were also known to have mental health problems. While this doesn't prove a causal association, it does add weight to my belief that places such as prisons need to be careful of encouraging already vulnerable minds to dwell on disturbing thoughts by writing too expressively. Even in 'normal' educational settings I have seen a clear association between highly gothic, bloodthirsty or fanciful writing with youngsters with the most fragile mental health. It isn't good enough to argue that they need an outlet for their feelings; what if the stimulation of such feelings is being boosted by the fact of the outlet?

It should be reasonably obvious that the more talent is supported by hard technical learning and practice, practice, practice, the more native genius shines through. Michelangelo, Shakespeare, Mozart – need I say more? It's going to be far better for a child (or adult in education, for that matter) to have greater flexibility with language and access to a choice of expressions which will help them to reproduce the voices and thought processes of a variety of people (not just the limited expressions, vocabulary and perspectives of their mates). Ironically, that flexibility is better achieved through more grammatical 'rules' (I know, dirty word), not fewer. It's about choice, not restriction, although restricting some language, according to the University of Reading, may be helpful.[8]

- Extreme or absolutist vocabulary, like extreme emotion, is associated with poorer mental health, so education can play its part by encouraging balance in language use: 'either/or', 'it is possible', 'although I believe', 'it can feel as if' and many other expressions can help to neutralise some of the inflexibility associated with various vulnerable mind states.

- At much the same time that grammar was being demoted and demonised, there was a trend in syllabus content and exam questioning to move away from the objective third person (which was insufficiently engaging) and towards the subjective first person.[9] Questioning in English language exams used to ask *why* and *how*, and instruct candidates to *explain, replace* and *precis,* all of which are designed to stimulate thought processes that use the logical (prefrontal, emotion regulating) and left-leaning (more positive) brain areas. More recent exam questions, although they still ask for technical awareness and

---

8   Mohammed Al-Mosaiwi, People with depression use language differently – here's how to spot it, *The Conversation* (2 February 2018). Available at: http://theconversation.com/people-with-depression-use-language-differently-heres-how-to-spot-it-90877.

9   Remember the mental health benefits of third-person language (see p. 38).

understanding (I don't want to oversell the point), lean more towards the student's personal and/or emotional experience of, and response to, the text. This expressive engagement may not be quite as positive in its impact as theorists once hoped, so let's encourage more objectivity in syllabuses to tilt things towards the optimistic part of the brain.

- Another baby and bathwater topic is learning by heart. Long considered to be 'education by Mr Gradgrind', it has been rescued from its dire reputation by Dr Helen Abadzi, cognitive psychologist and for twenty-seven years education specialist at the World Bank.[10] She has pointed out the importance of learning facts and creating automaticity to the development of analytic thinking, which she says is vital to making good decisions. Rejecting calls to do away with books and homework, and concerned that technology use is leading to confusing and unhelpful multitasking, Dr Abadzi says: 'Those who practise the most forget the least over time. So-called "overlearning" protects from forgetting, because consolidation requires repetition – small bits learned at a time.' Learning poetry by heart is a brilliant way to build up cognitive reserve; it is about banking information and ideas for the future.

Being careful about language use and being conscious of putting it together in a selective way – these things aren't just the obsessions of boring old grammar farts. Language matters because it is one of the most important building blocks of personality, and did I also mention that when it is used with imaginative flair it is something you can get high on?[11]

---

10 See Nicola Woolcock, Learning by heart is better for brain, *The Times* (31 October 2016).

11 At first sight this may seem like a contradiction to a lot of what I've written about free-flowing creative writing, but imaginative flair can be applied to a list of cake ingredients – try it for yourself! Note, however, what I have to say about dopamine and schizophrenia in Chapter 7.

Up and down and round and round we go

In this chapter we will look at the impact that a number of chemical substances have on us. After a saccharine desert, this will take us back into the realms of sugary loveliness, bloated emotions and big fat unexpected outcomes.

You might reasonably think that I'm going to be discussing heroin, cocaine, cannabis, alcohol and nicotine, possibly even coffee or sugar itself – all those alluring, compelling and thoroughly addictive substances which make life exciting but also ramp up the activity of the crazies in our brains. Although I will be touching on some of these substances, the chemicals I really want to get you thinking about are the ones that are impacted on by those external (or exogenous) substances.[1] I want to introduce you to the chemicals that you produce inside yourself, regardless of whether or not you indulge in a bit of exogenous activity. These are called endogenous chemicals and your state of mind is completely dependent on them, even if it's dependent on nothing else.

Briefly, if you think of these chemicals (also known as neurotransmitters or hormones) as messengers which carry instructions to and from various regions of the brain, with each one specialising in certain areas and activities, then you won't go far wrong. There is *serotonin* which carries instructions affecting pain, sleep and mood; *noradrenaline* which carries instructions affecting physical and mental arousal and mood; and *acetylcholine* which carries instructions affecting attention, memory and learning. There are many more, including dopamine and oxytocin which we will explore in more detail in the following pages, but as neurotransmitters are usually multi-talented and multi-functional there is much overlapping of chemicals and brain-related functions.

---

1   An exogenous chemical is one that originates outside the body. Those produced within the body are called endogenous.

Bodily health is a complicated enough matter to try to explain, but brain health makes it look like a playground-level activity. There are clearly thousands of factors involved – ranging from the extremely simplified version of brain regions which I have offered up with my model of hot-hatch drivers and classical goddesses, to the vats of chemical messenger soups into which I'm about to dive.

For the sake of simplicity, I'm going to focus primarily on the neurotransmitters which I believe tell the best story about how our brains generate the emotions which appear to be driving many of the mental health problems highlighted earlier in the book. Although serotonin (popularly referred to as the 'happiness hormone') is a really interesting hormone when it comes to brain health, I want to concentrate mostly on dopamine and oxytocin, both of which are often known by taglines which are neither particularly helpful nor accurate (mostly in the breathless and excitable media).

Dopamine is also referred to as a 'happiness hormone', which is even less appropriate than it is for serotonin. Oxytocin is variously called the 'cuddle hormone', the 'love hormone' or the 'empathy hormone' – again, not especially appropriate once we get into the reality of how it affects us. But these terms stick, and people have some strange ideas about what such hormones might be able to do for us, as though, rather than being simple chemical messengers they were some kind of behavioural/emotional Deliveroo service.

Here I will outline the bare bones of what these two chemicals actually do.

Dopamine

- Dopamine motivates and is involved in goal-directed behaviour. It is the chemical for significance and significance-seeking behaviour. However, paying attention and finding significance in things are not especially moral behaviours.
- Too much or too little dopamine in the system can lead to difficulties. Some forms of schizophrenia are marked by too much, while Parkinson's disease is marked by too little, resulting in inertia and immobility. (Gambling and sex compulsions have been some of the more curious and unexpected side effects of

certain chemical treatments which boost dopamine in Parkinson's patients.)

- Dopamine systems are involved in addiction. Variations in the ability to process dopamine, probably due to genetic mutations, are thought to be behind many cases.

- Dopamine needs to be at optimal levels for healthy functioning. Quick shifts in levels can be destabilising, often leading to mental problems.

- Dopamine is involved in language production but not necessarily in language logic. (Some forms of schizophrenia involve lots of language but rather less coherence – for example, 'word salad' and neologisms.)

- Producing dopamine can be a motivation in itself, leading to dopamine 'chasing'. It is associated with novelty, reward and arousal, but not necessarily with prosocial or moral behaviour.

The jury is out on how much dopamine levels can be affected by lifestyle choices. Some people appear to have genetically low levels; often, if they do not have sufficient self-discipline in place, they will find it very hard to reject substances which appear to be boosting their dopamine supplies, even if it's only a short-term effect. Learning to live with modest levels of satisfaction may be the only long-term solution for individuals in this situation, as most of dopamine-enhancing possibilities – drugs, alcohol, risky behaviour and so on – are either dangerous or addictive, or both. Perhaps it's the way that full-on, 24/7 party lives are marketed that makes us think we're missing out if we accept lower key living.

Oxytocin

- Oxytocin is the so-called 'cuddle hormone' that comes with rather dark benefits.

- It is produced by mothers going into labour and encourages lactation and bonding. (Oxytocin's association with human pair bonding and empathy was the outcome of research into pair bonding in prairie voles![2])

---

2   Sue Carter, The biology of 'love': lessons from prairie voles, *Open Access Government* (2 April 2019). Available at: https://www.openaccessgovernment.org/prairie-voles/62218.

- The use of oxytocin in treating people with autism spectrum disorders may be of benefit in terms of boosting empathy and closer emotional relationships, but the jury is still out on its effectiveness.

- A combination of higher than usual levels of both dopamine and oxytocin is probably behind the phenomenon we call 'romantic love'.

- Oxytocin is produced in closely bonded groups, leading to a sense of belonging and to 'in-groups'. It therefore leads to the creation of 'out-groups' – who are not at all bonded to the in-groups, nor approved of by them. Bonding is not necessarily moral but it feels good. When an in-group is not big on intimacy or prosocial behaviour, the outcome is not always pleasant.

- Racism, xenophobia and anti-social behaviour can easily be the outcome of plentiful supplies of oxytocin, as they are all examples of one group setting itself against other groups.

Oxytocin may or may not be the answer to human closeness; it's not yet been proven. But whether it is or isn't, there is no reason to see closeness as an unalloyed good per se – the Mafia may well be very bonded. When self-belief creeps in and people feel good about the group, then self-righteous pomposity and inflexibility can be the result, which is not good for mental health.

The reality is that actually we're all doing substances, all the time. Sometimes, quite often in fact, we behave in rather questionable ways as a consequence of being in their endogenous grip. If we add in yet more substances, the ones that come with their very own special relationships with ones we made earlier, then all sorts of problems can follow.

We will take a look at all of this shortly, but first we need to check out the implications of some of the things we've just discovered about dopamine and oxytocin because they have real implications for our mental health.

For a fuller working out of the ideas that follow, including the supporting research, I have to point you in the direction of *The Significance Delusion*. What follows here are some thoughts which were prompted, in part, by exploring the socially fascinating outcomes of what we normally refer to as the Black Death. However, I like to refer to it as the 'Black Birth', not just because I'm contrary, but because there is an argument to be made that the horrible events of that time had an unlooked for but positive consequence – that is, much greater social mobility and the effective social enfranchisement of many people who had previously been locked into very low-grade and servile lives.

Dopamine appears to have played a large part in what took place. Without following all the ins and outs of my arguments about medieval times, what is interesting here and now is that there are strong links between higher social status and greater numbers of dopamine receptors in the brain.[3] These, in turn, are associated with greater social support for the lucky high-status person. Perhaps unsurprisingly, this goes hand in hand with a link between lower social status and fewer dopamine receptors, and both with lower levels of social support.

Lots of questions inevitably follow such findings, but apart from wondering if high achievers might gain kudos from maintaining a distance from the 'lower ranks' (i.e. social out-groups) rather than drawing them into their wider social circles, and speculating on where that fits into the picture, we will move on to the question of mental health.

If the brains of individuals with lower social status have lower dopamine levels (and the numbers of receptors aren't absolute evidence for this but are fairly indicative) then they will also be less motivated in a number of ways, quite possibly seeing fewer rewards and incentives in prosocial behaviour, leading to anti-social or self-sabotaging lifestyles. It's a possibility at least, and we know that such lifestyles are strongly associated with poorer mental health. We also know that individuals with higher numbers of dopamine receptors enjoy better mental health, so it seems a no-brainer (or a bigger brainer, depending on your point of view).

But (and isn't there always a 'but'? – a word that we now know is in itself indicative of complex and mentally healthful and flexible thinking) you can have too much of a good thing. High dopamine levels, as well as promoting focus and goal-directed behaviour, can also fix attention on our own inner processes, leading to an inflated sense of self and overblown levels of self-belief, self-importance and general grandiosity.

---

3   Receptors are in effect docking stations for neurotransmitters, and the more receptors there are, the more chemical activity there can potentially be. For more on this see *The Significance Delusion*.

We all know people who dream the impossible dream, who have sweeping ambitions (with little obvious talent) and who set themselves crazy and unrealisable goals. And only too often, in this age of TV talent shows, ideologues and motivational speakers (not to mention advertising campaigns for teachers), too many people are actively encouraged to believe that if you 'aim for the stars' then 'nothing should hold you back' and 'you can achieve anything you want to achieve'. Sadly, overdosing on dopamine does not talent make, nor genuine achievement. But it can make for some unstable and even bipolar-type thought processes. Which is sad, and sadness is often the flip side of having been built up too much by dopamine rushes.

Bipolarity, whether it's formally diagnosed or more of a characteristic or tendency, comes with peaks and troughs of dopamine and excitability. This can make life unmanageable at times, and not only for the person involved. They can't always be depended on to follow through on things and their mood may change, often on a whim – all of which is hard for other people to handle and can lead to them becoming isolated and lonely, despite their manic moments of hyper-sociability.

This is why people who know they may be at the mercy of dopamine ups and downs should get on the best possible terms with their prefrontal cortex. If you have that cool classical character watching out for you, explaining your mood swings as they happen and keeping a checklist of the things you can do (which your best moments have told you will work) to stabilise your hormones, then you are in the best possible place to cope with whatever life throws at you.[4]

Like dopamine, oxytocin can have strange and unexpected effects when it comes to brain health. Apart from the way it can affect social bonds, it also impacts on our romantic attachments and entanglements. But try not to get too excited, because when engulfed by oxytocin you might find yourself in the grip of a passion for someone (or something) unlovely, which you might come to regret in a cold sweat of embarrassment. Pretty much as Titania does when she falls for Bottom the 'ass' in *A Midsummer Night's Dream*.

---

4   See again, *Touched with Fire* by Kay Redfield Jamison, on her strategies for dealing with her own manic depression. Manic depression was an earlier name for bipolar disorder.

Oxytocin can affect our judgement, making us more trusting, more accepting of other people (if they belong to the category of in-group), more approachable and more sociable. It can also, rather less pleasantly, lead to gloating over rivals and jealousy when losing out on something or someone. Trusting people who may not be trustworthy, finding the deeply unattractive desirable, and feeling competitive and jealous are some of the less lovely aspects of oxytocin production. But put it together with dopamine, generated in commitment to a cause, and you get some very dodgy possibilities indeed. How about:

- Absolute, unwavering belief in an ideology (however imperfect), probably communicated in some very absolutist language which leaves no room for nuance or adjustment.

- Deep hatred and anger towards out-groups – that is, anyone who doesn't subscribe to your ideology.

- Total trust in in-group members, especially high-status ones, and an inability to see anything unattractive or unreasonable in them or their behaviour.

- Becoming almost orgasmic on rectitude (and isn't that one of the sweetest tastes of all?). Hardly surprising then that so many teenagers, whose brains can be a bit all over the place and low on prefrontal activity, get high and emotionally bloated on this sugary hit.

It's small wonder that there is such a complicated two-way relationship between cults, causes and mental health difficulties.

It's a myth that empathy, the apparent outcome of having lots of bonding oxytocin, is an unalloyed good, either for the person doing the empathising or for everything and everyone with whom they empathise. Sold to us as leading to a more harmonious society, greater emotional intelligence, better working environments and more successful relationships, in reality, empathy (and its cousin emotional intelligence) may well have been something that Adolf Hitler had in spades. How else was he able to rouse, influence and manipulate his audiences? Knowing how others are feeling doesn't necessarily mean you care about those feelings, particularly if you're a sociopath.

Too much emotion in the workplace can be a bad thing, too, as it can lead to burnout. It has been pointed out that empathy can be a very overrated skill in medicine: over-identification with a patient can blur appropriate professional boundaries, and it can also be exhausting, leading to worse care and worse outcomes. Sometimes skilful, thoughtful objectivity and distance is the more caring approach.

It's also possible for empathy to be overly subjective, meaning the feeling is actually for the self rather than for the client/patient/friend/lover. It's back to I, myself and me. For the person being empathised with, it can feel as if they are being hijacked: 'If *you* are so full of me and what I'm going through, where am *I* in all of this?' Such sensitivity to others can be both a bit me, me, me and a bit pointless. What does it matter if you can feel my pain, what can you *do* for me? Sometimes brisk sympathy and practical help can be a better option than overdosing on oxytocin.

Other substances

If our brains can do so many zany things simply ramped up (or down) on self-generated chemicals, how much more can they do when fuelled by additional substances which work by hijacking the systems that are there to manage the barely house-trained endogenous ones?

The answer is quite a lot. Even legal psychoactive substances like coffee and sugar alter the way we think and feel (a huge part of their attraction), and they barely touch the sides of the chemical systems they affect, at least by comparison with some of the others. Nicotine, another (still just about) legal substance, has quite unusual effects, being both an upper and a downer. Mostly what we get addicted to with smoking tobacco is the need to prevent withdrawal, and that tells us quite a lot about how addiction works.

The chemicals in substances that we add to our already vulnerable neurotransmitter systems – and as mentioned earlier, the people most at risk of developing long-term and damaging 'addictions' (I don't really like that word, especially now that it seems to have become tainted by some rather bizarre romanticism in certain parts of the media) are those whose baseline settings for dopamine are probably already either low or variable[5] – can be so attractive that users either end up forever chasing the high or low that they get from them, or forever escaping the withdrawal effect of having to live without that high or low. Neither outcome produces what they want in the long run, and so they do more and more of whatever it is, to less and less effect.

Addiction isn't a permanent state: US soldiers who appeared to be addicted to heroin while in Vietnam – creating panic in the government at the prospect of their return – most often gave up their habit very quickly once they had family, prospects and hope back in their lives. Huge sighs of governmental relief. Nor is it inevitable. It's the outcome of a complex backstory of genetics, epigenetics (including parents' and grandparents' histories and lifestyles), upbringing, education, culture, environment and availability of materials.

That is a very small nutshell into which I've managed to cram the massive body of work on addiction, but what the heck! I will give you an equally speedy version of the mental health consequences of using just some of these substances. As 74 million sites come up when you google 'heroin', I don't think I can cover enough in this modest book to give much sage advice about many substances, but I hope to surprise you just a little bit with the few I do touch on.

Nicotine

Even when inhaled from an e-cigarette, nicotine is associated with hyperactivity in children born to users (admittedly the work involved mice, but so does a lot of medical research that over time is shown to be relevant to humans).[6] Nicotine is also a thoroughly toxic substance and, theoretically, too much of it could kill you.

---

5   People who have a genetic defect in the dopamine D2 inhibitory auto-receptor are described as having 'reward deficiency syndrome' – that is, they do not get normal levels of pleasure out of life's experiences. The D2R2 allele (variation) is found in up to 80% of alcohol- and drug-addicted people, as opposed to approximately 25% of the normal population. It is also associated with risky behaviours in general. See, for example, David Comings and Kenneth Blum, Reward deficiency syndrome: genetic aspects of behavioral disorders, *Progress in Brain Research* 126 (2000): 325–341.

6   Yvaine Ye, Nicotine exposure in male mice may trigger ADHD in their offspring, *New Scientist* (16 October 2018). Available at: https://www.newscientist.com/article/2182614-nicotine-exposure-in-male-mice-may-trigger-adhd-in-their-offspring.

Smoking by grandmothers during pregnancy has been associated with autism in grandchildren (the risk for granddaughters increased by 53% if a grandmother had smoked[7]); smoking by parents with miscarriage, prematurity, low birth weight, sudden infant death syndrome, asthma, bronchitis, ADHD and substance abuse of various kinds; and smoking by teens with alcohol and cannabis abuse and a twenty-two times greater risk of cocaine abuse[8] – teen use of any of which is in itself associated with poorer mental health.

Smoking by adults is associated with lung cancer and other lung diseases, as well as with heart disease, fertility problems and many other physical health problems. It is also correlated with poor decision-making, because knowing what risks may be involved in various situations and behaviours (not necessarily associated with smoking), smokers still choose to ignore them and make decisions which overlook their best interests[9] (quelle surprise!).

It's no wonder that smokers also have poorer mental health in general. The illusory effect that smoking nicotine calms people down (in care settings, for example) is particularly unkind, as the evidence shows that, in fact, after a tiny and short-lived benefit to nerves, the anxiety kicks in: 'How can I live without it, and when can I have my next one?' What smoking really does is to make the smoker more anxious and more agitated. Stopping smoking has been shown to have at least the same beneficial effect on anxiety and depression as taking antidepressants.[10] But we can't deny someone their only pleasure, can we? Not in this doggedly self-pleasuring society, anyway.

7   Jean Golding, Genette Ellis, Steven Gregory, Karen Birmingham, Yasmin Iles-Caven, Dheeraj Rai and Marcus Pembrey, Grandmaternal smoking in pregnancy and grandchild's autistic traits and diagnosed autism, *Scientific Reports* 7, article 46179 (2017). DOI: 10.1038/srep46179.

8   US Department of Health and Human Services, *The Health Consequences of Smoking. A Report of the Surgeon General* (Rockville, MD: US Department of Health and Human Services, Public Health Service, Office of the Surgeon General, 2004).

9   Pearl H. Chiu, Terry Lohrenz and P. Read Montague, Smokers' brains compute, but ignore, a fictive error signal in a sequential investment task, *Nature Neuroscience* 11(4) (2008): 514–520.

10 Gemma Taylor, Ann McNeill, Alan Girling, Amanda Farley, Nicola Lindson-Hawley and Paul Aveyard, Change in mental health after smoking cessation: systematic review and meta-analysis, *BMJ* 348 (2014): g1151.

Cannabis

Cannabis is another substance that some people seem weirdly keen to believe is either harmless or actively good for you. Having worked for a few years in drug and alcohol treatment settings in prisons, I can say for certain that there are innumerable people in custody who would not be there but for cannabis, and many of them know it. They are such a sad bunch. As one lad said, 'Don't ever let anyone tell you that cannabis isn't addictive. They've not been inside my head.'

Even if cannabis isn't chemically addictive (in the way that, say, heroin is), it has an exogenous effect (although that is not absolutely clear-cut) that is chemically addictive in terms of the effect it has on the endogenous system, and, probably for that reason, it is certainly psychologically and behaviourally addictive. What many people do not realise is how long cannabis traces stay in the body. This is an inexact science and variable from person to person, but as a very rough guide: LSD stays in the system for approximately three hours, alcohol and heroin for twelve hours, cocaine for around two days, but cannabis – anywhere from *two to four weeks*! How can it be totally neutral in effect?

Cannabis use in teenagers is associated with depression (short and long term), other mental health problems such as anxiety, short-term memory loss (which inevitably leads to poor academic performance: if there is no short-term acquisition of information, there is no long-term storage of it either) and inability to control behaviour.[11]

It is also associated in very vulnerable brains (of any age) with the possibility of permanent states of psychosis. Short-term psychosis is a more regular and relatively frequent outcome, but one that brings huge implications for society (crime, NHS costs, etc.) as well as for the individual involved.[12] Perhaps as a consequence of this, cannabis is also associated with accelerated brain ageing. But it's not alone in that – the same is true for alcohol and for various states that involve scattergun thinking, such as schizophrenia, bipolar disorder and ADHD, which are low on prefrontal control.

---

11 BBC News, Cannabis 'more harmful than alcohol' for teen brains (3 October 2018). Available at: https://www.bbc.co.uk/news/health-45732911.

12 Michelle Roberts, Potent cannabis increases risk of serious mental illness, says study, *BBC News* (20 March 2019). Available at: https://www.bbc.co.uk/news/health-47609849.

You have been warned: the prefrontal cortex is a great preserver of brains. Use yours to avoid cannabis! Exposure to cannabis also alters the genetic profile of sperm which has implications for future generations – you have been warned!

Alcohol

Alcohol is the final substance I will discuss in any detail. This is not a book specifically about addiction or addictive substances, so what I'm hoping to do here is to alert you to how very delicate and vulnerable our brains are to abuse of all kinds. And also how important it is to use our clear-thinking brain to make sensible decisions around using substances that might have the short-term desirability of, say, a big fat sugary dollop of emotional or physical pleasure but the long-term impact of screwing around with our brains.

A few examples which highlight what psychoactive substances are capable of should, I hope, stand for all. If the drugs I'm focusing on – which in various circles are considered to be pretty harmless if not outright okay – can do all that I say, what are the likely results (especially on the brain) of using crack cocaine, heroin, crystal meth, ecstasy or a whole raft of newer cooked-up chemical highs? This isn't about the individual effects of particular substances, so much as the principles around how we treat ourselves and how this affects others.

So, back to alcohol. It's been known for a long time that alcohol affects the unborn child, and in the worst cases severely affects brain development, but it is less well known that it also leads to miscarriage in women and reduced fertility in men. And, like cannabis, alcohol use may affect the way genetic information gets passed down the generations, meaning that we simply don't know how heavy alcohol use in a grandparent might have affected the brain development of a grandchild.[13] Ultimately, we're all responsible for the brain health of our species.

Alcohol is a depressant, and that sometimes surprises people because lots of us appear super-happy on alcohol, at least for a time. For most people the more they drink, the more morose they become. There is a reason for this: what gets depressed by alcohol first is our

---

13 Again, this is the area of science called epigenetics. It is becoming ever clearer that the way genetic information gets passed on is not fixed, but is affected by environmental factors which include the health and behaviour of all generations.

usual layer of inhibition (very British), and so with our inhibition down we let rip with our laughter, our larynxes and our behaviour in general. We're not necessarily having a good time; what we're actually having is a less psychologically corseted time. Unless we're naturally a very cheery person in the first place, the chances are that we will go on to express all our normally nipped in and suppressed anger, depression and misery as the night goes on.

Anyone who has ongoing depression, anxiety, grief, low self-esteem and so on is much more likely to feel worse with alcohol, not better. Need I add that the first thing to go with alcohol use (as with nearly all substances) is the self-knowledge and self-awareness which the prefrontal cortex gives us, so we're always the last one to know how daft and miserable we're being. The hot-hatch boy is in charge, but he's having a bit of a breakdown himself.

All substances of potential abuse work by targeting the same pathways and receptors on which our endogenous brain chemicals rely. Some drugs appear to boost the levels of naturally occurring chemicals, and some (such as ecstasy) artificially boost the neurotransmitter serotonin to such an extent that the body effectively can't be bothered to make the effort any more and stops producing enough. The highs of ecstasy often lead to deep and ongoing depression. If we always depend on artificial means to feel good, to feel better than we did, to stop feeling so bad or to feel completely other than we were, we also run the risk of losing touch with reality (potentially forever) and losing out on who we might have been in a more natural and authentic way.

Finally, do we need a whole societal rethink about what it means to have a 'drugs problem'? I'm aware of a case in a prison where a trained drugs worker, employed by the NHS, refused treatment to a prisoner on the basis that 'he does not have any problematic drug problems', despite the fact that he was found in possession of 11 grams of cocaine (1.2 grams of cocaine can be lethal) and 8 grams of cannabis (for which he received a sentence of nine months) as well as a prohibited weapon (a further two years). If this is the sort of jumbled logic that a specialist drugs and alcohol worker can come up with, then what will it take for the rest of us to understand the true implications of messing about with our brains?

Parents' takeaway for protecting youngsters against substance-related problems

- Pregnant women should avoid alcohol, nicotine, cannabis and all other non-medically recommended drugs. All are associated with risks to the baby's developing brain. Apart from the direct risks, there is also an association between a mother's smoking and later substance use by the child.[14] Both grandmaternal and maternal smoking are likely to produce epigenetic changes in genes which will affect brain function in many ways and will almost certainly impact on future generations.

- Would-be fathers should stop smoking because smoking (even pre-puberty) can affect sperm in potentially harmful ways.[15] Similarly, their alcohol intake is nearly as important to their future children's brain health as their mother's – if too high it can affect a baby's brain size and development. If very high it can lead to foetal alcohol disorder in the newborn – even if the mother has not drunk at all.

- It's a myth that introducing children to small amounts of alcohol early helps them to drink sensibly. No alcohol in childhood works best for that.

- Be a good role model and don't think that being a chillaxed kind of parent who does a few lines of coke or a few puffs of weed won't affect them.[16] It will. Not only will it normalise

---

14 The Conversation, Smoking during pregnancy may lead to later substance use in the child (6 December 2016). Available at: http://theconversation.com/smoking-during-pregnancy-may-lead-to-later-substance-use-in-the-child-69929.

15 Kate Northstone, Jean Golding, George Davey Smith, Laura Miller and Marcus Pembrey, Prepubertal start of father's smoking and increased body fat in his sons: further characterisation of paternal transgenerational responses, *European Journal of Human Genetics* 22(12) (2014): 1382–1386; Jonathan Day, Soham Savani, Benjamin Krempley, Matthew Nguyen and Joanna Kitlinska, Influence of paternal preconception exposures on their offspring: through epigenetics to phenotype, *American Journal of Stem Cells* 5(1) (2016): 11–18.

16 I'm with Cressida Dick, Commissioner of the Metropolitan Police Service, on this one. Cool, usually middle-class, parents can be utterly hypocritical about cocaine use, totally ignoring its social impact and its international trail of environmental, cultural and personal harm, so long as they see it as part of their inalienable right to their 'lifestyle'. See Haroon Siddique, Middle-class cocaine users are hypocrites, says Met chief, *The Guardian* (31 July 2018). Available at: https://www.theguardian.com/society/2018/jul/31/middle-class-cocaine-users-are-hypocrites-says-met-chief-cressida-dick.

neediness, but it will also set up double standards – and that's pretty confusing for a developing brain.

○ Another myth is that the best way to protect against drug use is to give young people more information about substances and lifestyle, so they can make better and more informed choices. In reality, according to Drug and Alcohol Findings, 'Child development and parenting programmes which do not mention substances at all (or only peripherally) have recorded some of the most substantial prevention impacts.'[17] The Rotterdam-based programme which prompted this assertion is only one piece of evidence that supports the idea that substance use is fundamentally an outcome of background, environment, parenting and social tolerance. Further confirmation comes from Iceland, where the Youth in Iceland programme has reportedly radically reduced teen substance abuse with its package of sports involvement (contractually obligatory), parental engagement, youth curfews and purposeful activities.[18] Neither initiative primarily focuses on teaching young people about substances and their risks, but they implicitly recognise that building better and more resilient brains is the best way to get those brains to make better and more prefrontally biased choices. Truly cool classical control!

Educators' takeaway for protecting youngsters against substance-related problems

○ The previous section is as relevant to education as it is to parenting, and it shows that involvement in sports is hugely helpful in steering children away from less desirable activities. Sport, and exercise in general, is one of the best ways to get the natural high that so many people try to imitate through drugs and risky behaviours. Thankfully, most schools are coming round to recognising this. (Again, past centuries and civilisations understood it very well!)

---

17 Drug and Alcohol Findings, Hot topics. It's magic: prevent substance use problems without mentioning drugs (23 January 2017). Available at: https://findings.org.uk/PHP/dl.php?file=hot_no_drugs.hot.

18 See https://planetyouth.org.

- People with more 'cognitive capital' are not only better protected from dementia and its effects, but they are also better protected against the adverse effects of poor lifestyles, (including drug and alcohol use). The reasons are complex but, put simply, the greater the level of education, the better chance someone has of getting clean or of avoiding long-term physical damage. This may well be down to the greater numbers of connections between neurons which ultimately help the brain to make better ongoing decisions.

- Science lessons can be very helpful in developing youngsters' understanding of the interplay between brain, chemicals and physical and emotional behaviour (see Youth in Iceland again). It's not so much that teaching *facts* about drugs works to prevent juvenile experimentation, but that learning about matters like exogenous and endogenous chemicals and their importance in our mental life not only helps children to get a wider perspective on all human experience, but it also helps them to understand their own experiences much better.

- This may also be helpful to them in recognising how advertising and social media can impact on brain chemistry to make them do things their prefrontal cortices would find daft. Here is an opportunity for science lessons and sociology/psychology/ business studies to combine forces and demonstrate how complex human behaviour really is.

- Both chemistry and cookery classes can help young people to explore the impact of different substances on the body. Sugar is not so very different from cocaine in some of its effects, and a recognition that just about everything we do to ourselves can change the way we think or act is as fascinating as it is thought-provoking to children. This is as much about filling them with enthusiasm for joined-up learning as it is about me sending out negative messages.

- Protecting young people is not necessarily about teaching them facts about drugs, which was the approach of one college where I worked. At a staff drugs awareness day I was one of only two lecturers who didn't 'do' drugs or find them acceptable as a simple fact of life. Many attendees simply seemed to want to show off their own streetwise credentials. Much of what I've written above should perhaps be applied to those in charge of other people's children as well as to the children themselves. As ever, modelling desired behaviours is one of adults' most powerful tools.

- My final piece of advice to people of all ages is: your brain should not be a laboratory for whacky chemical experiments – it has enough problems of its own!

Chapter 8

The less sweet sweet spot

At the end of Chapter 2, I suggested that it has to be easier to adjust our expectations than to change the world, but I think that the idea might be something of a challenge to the generations who have been brought up to believe in the absolute primacy of what they think of as Rights and Social Justice. For thousands, if not millions (given the huge impact of social media), it is an unquestionable assumption that dedication to these gods is not so much a Good Thing, as a religious calling. And as feelings are very much at the heart of any calling, the link is pretty clear: we feel greater than good when we are called on to serve a cause.[1]

As this book aims to challenge some well-rooted assumptions, in order to get to the bottom of what works to promote better mental health, I'm going to look at some areas that have recently been surrounded by such a celestial light that we have not dared to direct our eyes towards them lest we be blinded. It's not that I'm actually criticising social justice or even rights (without capital letters); it's the assumptions that have been made about them that I'm questioning.

The assumption I'm making in this book is that we want to have a mentally healthier population – meaning a whole lot of *people*, not a *thing* called Society. I'm going to take a pop at a few sacred cows, and then suggest that achieving better mental health may be easier and quicker if we go for the 'sweet spot', the Goldilocks option, that lies somewhere between achieving a perfect society and having absolutely inalienable individual rights (surely an oxymoron).

First in the line of fire has to be, ironically, the sweetness of rectitude, because getting to the Goldilocks sweet spot is about achieving the flexibility involved in compromise and pragmatism (and we already know that flexibility helps with mental health). If our number one priority is to be right, then that tends to come at the cost of

---

1 And religions have been known both to offer up unwilling sacrificial victims and encourage adherents to sacrifice themselves in the name of the greater good.

seeing the bigger picture.[2] Learning how to be, if not wrong as such, but more open to other points of view and different ways of going about things, is associated with wider and more extensive neural networks – in themselves indicative of both cleverer thinking and better mental health. We may have to cut back on the sugar as we open up thinking to alternative possibilities.

On the question of whether, in the cause of better mental health, it is going to be more effective to be prepared to change I, myself and  me and my expectations occasionally (just a wee bit), rather than going for the nuclear option of having to create that perfect world of total social justice which allows for every single ideological demand to be met, this strikes me as a somewhat conflicted option. One person's demand may cancel out another person's rights – for example, the freedom to smoke in a public place may put a pregnant woman at risk of secondary inhalation. By fulfilling insistent ideological demands (immediately, of course) we may, unwittingly, be creating bad outcomes for mental health by setting in stone as yet unproven – but unquestionable – assumptions about what makes for a Better Society.

So, to pose some contemporary, tricky, but pertinent to youngsters' mental health, questions, what about these sacred cows? What if:

- By aiming for equality of opportunity universities are unexpectedly becoming part of the mental health problem?
- By aiming for happiness we're unexpectedly ending up with unhappier people?
- By empowering single interest communities we're unexpectedly messing with people's brains?
- By aiming for the stars we're unexpectedly ending up in a mental midden?

Let's take these possibilities one at a time.

---

2   Autism is not a subject I'm going to go into in-depth in this book, but many people on the autism spectrum can be very single-minded, seemingly arrogant (lacking social skills that others may have) and believe strongly, even fixedly, in their own point of view. They can also get very cross when crossed. They often have a strange charisma which draws others to them and their fixed positions. They can also be very persuasive in public debate, especially when given their own unchallenged platform (naming no names). Their inability to adapt means they are at a higher than usual risk of developing psychological problems.

Universities

(This also applies to other institutions which are attempting to combine their primary cause for existence – in this case learning, which is also associated with preparation for a professional future – with a social justice target, such as social mobility, access or diversity.)

According to all the reports, whether from student charities, mental health organisations or universities themselves, students are struggling with stress like never before. Even at elite universities, where we might presume that those healthful, good thinking brain skills were prioritised, the problem has not been mitigated and is at least as bad (actually worse in some cases, suicide rates being horrifically high in some Russell Group universities – Bristol being a recent example[3]). Explanations are looked for in every corner of modern life, from high student fees to huge workloads to too much testing or insufficient mental health support. Insensitive older folk mutter about a snowflake generation.

But what if a large part of the problem is down to universities having set targets for equality, together with policies around students' rights, which in the race for rectitude completely ignore the reality of how brains and mental health work?[4]

Like brains, institutions need to be taking lots of matters into consideration and not allowing themselves to be hijacked by single fixations or red-hot causes. However, at the moment universities seem to be in the grip of a fever of virtue signalling, especially around equality, diversity and (some) students' inalienable Rights.

By focusing all their attention on getting more and more students from disadvantaged backgrounds, or disadvantaged groups, into higher education, both governments and institutions have lost sight of (or, more likely, never known or acknowledged in the first place) the realities of mental health.

---

3   Peter Stubley, Chemistry student dies suddenly in 13th suspected suicide at Bristol University in three years, *The Independent* (10 August 2019). Available at: https://www.independent.co.uk/news/uk/home-news/student-death-suicide-bristol-university-maria-stancliffe-cook-a9051606.html.

4   Having taken part in a number of professional conferences where student mental health was the main topic, I can whisper in your ear that many of the speakers were privately of the opinion that too much focus is placed on students' vulnerabilities and that essentially they need to toughen up. More than their campus-based jobs are worth, though …

It may taste very sweet to open up higher education to more and more teens, but what if:

- Their education to date has simply not given them either the skills or the knowledge to be able to cope with what is going to be thrown at them? Wishing a thing does not make it happen, and they are less likely to do well once exposed to better teaching and/or more aspirational peers than they are to feel pressured, inadequate and stressed out.

- Their education to date has promoted and prioritised teaching which (unknowingly) has led to vulnerability to mental problems? By this I mean focusing on the development of narrow, self-opinionated and feelings-driven thinking at the expense of broader, contextualised and objective thinking.

- They have pre-existing mental health problems – and many students self-identify as having them? (A thought: what should the role of families be in this respect?)

- They have been encouraged to apply because they think they should (perhaps to fulfil a target or ideology), rather than having either inclination or aptitude?

There are many other 'what ifs', and they may seem harsh at first sight, but I want to put the challenge out there. Such students are much more likely to have mental health difficulties while at university. They will be less resilient to stress and challenge,[5] and place more demands on mental health services. Who does this benefit? The anxious, depressed, unhappy student, who may have done better to take a different path in life or try university later when they were better prepared for the challenge,[6] or the institution, which can no longer place teaching and research at the forefront of what they do (their original remit), as they must focus on student wellbeing, which they are not specifically prepped for, nor qualified or adequately funded to do?

---

5   Certain types of events may be 'immunising' (i.e. stress inoculation, steeling effects) and exposure may have buffered the individual from the effects of stressful life events. Findings from the preclinical literature have demonstrated that certain doses of stress can protect organisms from having a high-stress reaction to adversity later in life: see Steven F. Maier, Jose Amat, Michael V. Baratta, Evan Paul and Linda R. Watkins, Behavioural control, the medial prefrontal cortex, and resilience, *Dialogues Clinical Neuroscience* 8(4) (2006): 397–406.

6   I spent many happy years teaching A levels to adults. Not only were these students some of the best and most motivated I have ever known, they were also (by and large) not unhappy to have left their studies till later.

It seems to me that, rather than completely rewriting the purpose of higher education, we would be in a sweeter place if we stopped just assuming that the social justice agenda leads to better mental well-being, and accepted a middle ground that entertains the possibility that not everyone is suited to higher education, especially when the chances are that their brains are either in some way unprepared or particularly vulnerable to stress, and that a university's primary function is to educate, not caretake. However, once a university or college has (with, dare I use the word, discrimination) taken a student on (even if not acting *in loco parentis*), they do have an absolute obligation to support students with their mental health and to both teach and run the institution in ways that promote, rather than harm, students' wellbeing.

Which neatly brings me on to … student activism. And a whole lot of trouble! Because we're back to two of my favourite things – the amygdala and silo, or single issue, thinking. And what I have to say is bound to rebound.

Single issue thinking, especially in activism, means both the inevitable boosting of the sense of the ultra-significance of 'the cause' and of the individual who believes in it, resulting in raised levels of dopamine and oxytocin (as discussed in the previous chapter), and the inflexibility of expecting the whole world to adapt itself to you while your thinking remains inviolate.

There is a danger in this way of seeing things. For a good and nuanced article on this topic, take a look at 'Don't let students run the university' by Tom Nichols.[7] It is biased towards the problem of student activism in the United States, which is closing down free speech and making demands which are all about the minority interest at the expense – metaphorically and literally – of other people who might have rights (small r) of their own, but it's a still a relevant and thought-provoking read for readers in the UK.

Nichols mentions the qualities which a university could be hoped to encourage in students – rigour, tolerance, commitment, self-discipline and courageous enquiry, but it seems that those are the

---

7   Tom Nichols, Don't let students run the university, *The Atlantic* (7 May 2019). Available at: https://www.theatlantic.com/ideas/archive/2019/05/camille-paglia-protests-represent-dangerous-trend/588859. See also a trenchant article by Kathryn Ecclestone, professor of education at the University of Sheffield, which looks at universities' possible over-sensitisation to students' emotional vulnerability: The effects of a 'vulnerability zeitgeist' in universities: real need or real life?, *University and College Counselling* 4(3) (2016): 4–9.

very qualities which the promotion of certain forms of activism that demand safe spaces and trigger warnings (no testing of tolerance, courageous enquiry or even of the self-discipline involved in keeping the anxiety or anger of the amygdala at bay) is most likely to kill off.

If students demand that the world must be made in their image or they will have to go away and hide, what does this mean for their mental health? No challenge, no stress inoculation, no flexibility of thinking, no exercise of brain function, too much emotional reaction and too little rational debate = more mental health vulnerability.

Is the toleration of intolerance of challenge and exposure to other people's perspectives by universities (and especially students' unions, as they are often the promoters of these divisions, in supposedly diverse institutions) really likely to support students' mental wellbeing? Wouldn't a Goldilocks sweet spot look more like a place where calm, rational and even formalised and disciplined debate could thrash out the multiple (because there never is just one matter at stake) issues behind differences? All done according to Queensberry Rules, of course, and all promoting the prefrontal classical saviour of the brain.

If universities are going to keep their place as centres of intellectual advancement and social mobility, then they may have to demonstrate rather more intellectual rigour themselves, promoting what works, rather than what they want to work. They may also have to be less tolerant of individual Rights and more tolerant of the rights of the many, who probably just want to work and get on with stuff that will help them into careers.

Happiness

Next, I want to consider happiness and its possible role in unhappiness. This is an awful association to make, given that there is now a supposed Right to happiness, but have we been getting it wrong? Should we be assuming that happiness is essential to humankind? After all, even the United States Declaration of Independence only suggests that people have inalienable rights to 'Life, Liberty and the *pursuit* of Happiness' (my italics), which is not remotely the same as saying that people have a right to happiness, never mind a Right.

Yet this assumption is practically built in to some educational and mental health ideologies, and happiness is now even taught as a subject in some schools.[8] There is a whole industry behind happiness lessons, which is dedicated to promoting the idea that happy schools get better results and happy pupils are mentally stronger.[9]

The aim of this section is not to knock happiness as such – I like to be happy, too – so much as to knock it off its top spot as a promoter of better mental health. There are many happily deluded people in the world, who usually don't do much for their families' wellbeing (mania can be extraordinarily cheerful, but it isn't necessarily careful of bank balances or the safety of the world around it), and there are countless fanatics who go smilingly to their doom, often taking less committed people with them.

It would be lovely – and, of course, very sweet – if we could all feel at one with ourselves and with everybody with whom we come into contact. But sometimes tension, stress and anger can be mightily motivating (a lot depends on the individual), and happy can feel a bit, well, aimless and dampish.

That is, unless it is motivated by anger and hatred. Apparently people are happier if they are able to feel the emotions they desire, even if they are unpleasant. A study carried out by a team of international researchers found that happiness is more than simply 'increasing pleasure and decreasing pain', and that the greatest life satisfaction was experienced by those whose emotions matched the ones they wanted.[10] Surprisingly, significant numbers of people prefer having negative rather than positive emotions.

Should they feel (and fear) that there is social pressure to want different ones? Especially as the study also concluded that in Western societies people experience a pressure to feel good, even better than they do already, and that can make them feel less happy overall. As another study suggested, feeling bad about feeling bad can make

---

8   Olivia Parker, Should happiness be part of the school curriculum?, *The Telegraph* (11 July 2016). Available at: https://www.telegraph.co.uk/education/2016/07/11/should-happiness-be-part-of-the-school-curriculum.

9   As noted earlier, adults can often confuse excitement and happiness, and make the assumption that squealing and screaming kids are happy ones. Not necessarily so. There is a hair's breadth between hyper-excitement, fear and anxiety. Calmer children are usually genuinely happier ones.

10 Maya Tamir, Shalom Schwartz, Shige Oishi and Min Kim, The secret to happiness: feeling good or feeling right?, *Journal of Experimental Psychology: General* 146(10) (2017): 1448–1459 at 1448. Available at: https://www.apa.org/pubs/journals/releases/xge-xge0000303.pdf.

you feel worse.[11] And yet another one, that chasing after happiness can make you feel that time is passing you by.[12] 'How much time is left for me to find perfect happiness? I haven't got enough left. Help!'

How about finding a middle ground of just about contented enough? This might take away the stress involved in having to be happy, and then perhaps schools can happily get back to promoting a neural network protecting perspective. And don't we all love Eeyore?

Single interest communities

It's not clear if people who are otherwise psychologically lost find the home they have been looking for in single interest communities of often quite varied types of people, or if, once again, it is the fact of belonging to a cause that results in the often narrow and unconnected thought processes which seem to be associated with adopting a single point of view. Emotional vulnerability does appear to be part of the picture. Could it be because by limiting our focus to one topic of interest, one presumed priority, one passion, there is an inevitable loss of the wider and more contextualised thinking which is known to be better for mental health?

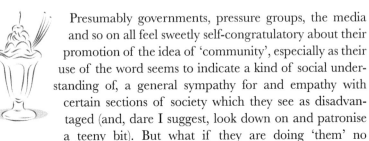 Presumably governments, pressure groups, the media and so on all feel sweetly self-congratulatory about their promotion of the idea of 'community', especially as their use of the word seems to indicate a kind of social understanding of, a general sympathy for and empathy with certain sections of society which they see as disadvantaged (and, dare I suggest, look down on and patronise a teeny bit). But what if they are doing 'them' no favours? Even the separation of 'them' is in itself a reason to worry, as it can (a) confer special status and (b) lead to silo thinking, which may ironically lead to 'them' feeling and being less agentic (assuming less responsibility for their actions) and having less of the

---

11 Brett Ford, Phoebe Lam, Oliver John and Iris Mauss, The psychological health benefits of accepting negative emotions and thoughts: laboratory, diary, and longitudinal evidence, *Journal of Personality and Social Psychology* 115(6) (2018): 1075–1092.

12 Aekyoung Kim and Sam Maglio, Vanishing time in the pursuit of happiness, *Psychonomic Bulletin & Review* 25(4) (2018): 1337–1342.

multifactorial, multilayered thinking which brings protection against mental health problems.[13]

I have suggested that the associations within single interest communities can be quite loose, involving various different types of people, some of whom may have no more in common than one core idea. There is nothing to promote the complex relationship building that comes with deep knowledge, a shared moral or ethical code and shared multilayered experiences, which is the foundation of really healthy communities. And, of course, there is no embedded interest in promoting or acknowledging the interests of those who are not in the in-group.

The single key idea can take over to such an extent that most other considerations (even of logic) get lost. As a thought experiment, I'm going to highlight some of the cognitive confusion that such decontextualised or silo thinking can lead to by taking one example from what has become known as Women's Issues. These have become more than a little divisive in recent times, so I'm possibly taking my life in my hands, but they affect most of us (after all, women do produce and raise men) and highlight in a reasonably accessible way what I think can go wrong when we lose sight of the bigger picture. I simply want to explore a couple of articles written by high-profile female writers in a respected publication, the *Sunday Times* Style section, and therefore probably taken as read by a lot of readers.

I'm not going to delve into the content of the articles, but simply quote parts of the biggest messages (literally) to which readers are exposed: the headlines (although these may not have been written by the journalist themselves). One piece has the heading, 'NU RAGE: Two new books champion the feminist power of being angry. Sick of being told to "Calm down, dear"? Pandora Sykes explores how to harness female fury for good.' The other, written by Dolly Alderton, reads, 'THE LIFE OF DOLLY: When it comes to being ghosted, our columnist has one piece of advice – track him down and find out the truth'.[14] It goes on to advise women to *force* a

---

13 This type of thinking allows that there are many things, in any situation or challenge, which need to be taken into consideration – all of which is associated with mental balance and better mental health.

14 See https://www.thetimes.co.uk/article/pandora-sykes-discusses-how-women-can-harness-their-collective-anger-for-good-ws5s6qj27 and https://www.thetimes.co.uk/article/what-happened-when-dolly-alderton-confronted-the-man-who-ghosted-her-883cthml0. Note: the headlines in the print editions differ slightly from the online versions.

man to meet up again in order to get an explanation and apology out of him.

Do I actually need to ask anyone to imagine the outcry if a man either wrote in this way about women or was effectively advising men to stalk a woman before forcing her to tell him what he wanted to hear? Is it that sweet sense of belonging to a specific group – in this case, a very cross and aggrieved group – that seems to make this acceptable? Because, if we're thinking about wider society, consistency and logic seem to have become absurdly compromised.

Another example of consistency and logic getting lost in the pursuit of principle comes from some feminist attitudes to language. In the UK it is believed that proper equality is achieved when women get to be known by the same names as men – as author, actor, police officer, where once they were, authoress, actress, policewoman. But in France, proper female equality has been achieved now that women can use feminised endings on previously masculine names (for example, *écrivaine* and *ingénieure* in place of *écrivain* and *ingénieur*). This is 'a big step for women', apparently.

By adopting, or even hijacking, the aggressive and despised language[15] and stances of anything or anyone we're aiming to challenge, what do we end up with? Contradictions and confusion. How can a brain compute all of this in a way that doesn't end up in some confusion? Except, of course, by simply ignoring any inconvenient counterarguments or positions.

This is rather difficult for a developing brain to do without causing some damage to long-term wellbeing, because small brains are searching for patterns and consistency to help them make sense of the world. When they fail to find regular, dependable models of how things work, they are likely to act out in higgledy-piggledy ways, leading to anxiety, depression, ADHD and even latent psychosis.

Take the case of a small child being brought up hearing that it's okay to be a strong and empowered woman, but that any talk of strength and power in connection to men is not really on. Where but in a state of confusion about what it takes to be either a man or a woman does that leave a growing brain? I'm not anti-feminist, so I

---

15 Or the tone – this is from the Chime for Change campaign for women, created by the renowned social activists at Gucci: 'We do not change the world when we whisper, we change it when we roar.'

must stress that the same principle applies with other, single issue, non whole-society centric thinking and groups.

Perhaps a sweeter sweet spot for women's issues might be found in taking a stand in the world of medical trials. It's one where traditionally no differentiation has been made, based on size or biological composition, in either testing or treatment. In other words, male and female physiologies have been regarded as indistinguishable – that is, default male – which is bonkers! Surely, wouldn't this be a much easier gender divide to acknowledge and make adjustments for without confusion, resentment or negative health implications?

Beam me up, Scottie!

Or, is aiming for the stars always the best thing for mental health?

When even Farrah Storr, editor of *Cosmopolitan* magazine, which traditionally encourages young women to aim for the stars in any and every area of life, admits that 'you can't have it all',[16] then perhaps it's time for us ordinary mortals to start questioning the assumption that having high ambitions is always a Good Thing.

This idea has been sold to us relentlessly, and carried home in bags emblazoned with motivational slogans such as, 'You can be anything you want to be', 'You're worth it', 'Live the dream', 'You're awesome', 'Your only limit is you', 'I'm going to make you so proud (note to self)' and other such factually questionable declarations. These affirmations may help with short-term commitment to a goal or ambition, but do they – can they – lead to genuine satisfaction in life?

Furthermore, is reaching for the stars in any way related to actual achievement?[17] For example, according to one survey (by Viga on behalf of financial services provider OneFamily) of just over 2,000 teens, on average they expected to be on salaries of around £70,000

---

16 Lucy Bannerman and Tatiana Hepher, You can't have it all, admits Cosmopolitan editor Farrah Storr, *The Times* (29 September 2019).

17 I was speaking to a group of Year 12s who were chatting about the careers they were looking into. One boy simply said, as though it was an end in itself, 'I can be anything I want to be.' Not wishing to dampen his enthusiasm too much, I simply pointed out that I (at five foot not very much and whatever age I then was) couldn't become a six-foot supermodel. He rather decently took my point. Is this a sensible notion for teachers to be promoting? And was teaching always *their* stellar ambition? If not …

at the age of 30. [18] On average, the reality is nearer to £23,000. Roughly half of them expected to have their dream job and to own their home in their twenties, and nearly a quarter to be running their own business. Nearly half expected to be married with families, and many to have travelled the world.

Clearly the stats do not stack up, but hope springs eternal in the bosom of youth. It is the job of adults to bring a little pragmatic reality into the equation (this actually happens in some parts of the world) to save young people the distress of disappointment, if nothing else. Because disappointment is more or less bound to happen to them according to the necessarily dull (but presumably gainfully employed) stats people at the Office for National Statistics (ONS).

In 2011 the ONS asked 16- to 21-year-olds what jobs they wanted to do, with many suggesting aspirational careers such as teacher, actor, doctor or firefighter. Six years later they followed up the participants and discovered that, apart from those who aimed to go into teaching (perhaps it really is a stellar ambition!), most teens' more aspirational job ambitions went west. The reality was that they had ended up with more lowly work in areas such as selling, caring or marketing. The higher the aspiration, the bigger the disappointment, too. By their late twenties (in 2017) only 1.4% had got media or arts jobs, such as producer, actor or writer; only 1.7% had got work in the police or emergency services; and approximately only 1.7% were employed as health professionals. [19]

Is it really kind to suggest that a child can be anything they want to be? Or is the kindness more self-centred and to do with adults feeling good about ourselves and our support for the young? Not to mention, of course, the hideous possibility that adults might have an interest in avoiding the sour taste of having to give out seemingly negative messages.

It appears that the situation might be even worse than the ONS stats suggest. According to an article on the BBC website, young people who set themselves ambitious goals, but then fail to achieve them in what they regard as a timely manner, now suffer from FOMOMG, or fear of missing out [on] my goals. Even though they may be

---

18 Sarah Young, Teenagers expect to earn triple the average salary by the time they turn 30, *The Independent* (13 February 2019). Available at: https://www.independent.co.uk/life-style/teenagers-salary-dream-job-work-career-survey-a8777151.html.

19 Sean Coughlan, How do career dreams really work out?, *BBC News* (27 September 2018). Available at: https://www.bbc.co.uk/news/education-45666030.

doing much better than average, they still aren't seeing their lives as successful. As one interviewee said, 'The worst thing for me is the internal pressure. When I feel I'm failing myself there's a frustration.'[20]

When you tell a young person they can be, do or achieve anything they want, you're placing a huge personal responsibility on them. Nothing is down to chance or to other people's interventions, it's all down to *you*. At which point you may shout, 'But you said be agentic, take responsibility!' To which I say, this chapter is about sweet spots – ones which in this case lie somewhere between the extremes of emotional self-indulgence and out-and-out, set-in-concrete pragmatism. Between perfectibility and harsh unrelenting reality.

The idea of perfectibility – that everything and everyone can reach such a state of grace that nothing more can be added or subtracted in order to make it better – goes back a very long way. You could argue that it is at the heart of a number of religious philosophies, particularly the religion that more people in the West seem to subscribe to than any formal faith: the religion of self-help and self-improvement.

Samuel Smiles, who wrote the original book on self-help, was a nineteenth-century reforming campaigner.[21] He argued that both bad government policies and foolish, unthrifty, personal behaviour led to poverty. His ambition was to create a better society through changing the more easily changeable – by helping individuals to make adjustments to their own lives. The book is still pertinent, but since those times the understanding of the phrase 'self-help' has changed quite a bit, becoming more solipsistic and self-serving at the expense of the greater social purpose Smiles had in mind.

Today self-help and self-improvement are more usually associated with perfecting the personal life; an aim which is just about as achievable as most career dreams and about as mentally healthful as you might imagine. I will come to issues surrounding body perfectionism in Chapter 9, but here I will just touch on the downsides associated with expecting that life should be perfect.

20 Cherry Wilson, We have FOMOMG – do you?, *BBC News* (22 October 2018). Available at: https://www.bbc.co.uk/news/uk-45894506.

21 Samuel Smiles, *Self-Help; With Illustrations of Character and Conduct* (London: John Murray, 1859).

According to one study which looked into the attitudes of over 41,000 British, American and Canadian college students between 1989 and 2016, the more the students were preoccupied with perfecting their lives, the more they experienced dissatisfaction as a result.[22] Dissatisfaction can be the forerunner to anxiety-related disorders; as ever, fixation on any extreme is the opposite of the flexible mindset that we know helps to maintain good brain health. As Graham Greene observed, 'Despair is the price one pays for setting oneself an impossible aim.'[23]

According to another study reported in *The Times*, some aspects of a belief in perfectibility may actually end up damaging the already least perfect lives the most.[24] Apparently, poorer American children, who had been encouraged to believe that the educational system was fair and that if they worked hard they could achieve anything, though very well behaved at 11, were more likely to lose faith and start to behave worse over the following two years – when ideal met real. As the study's lead, Erin Godfrey, put it, 'You're pitting two different cognitions against each other.'

Of course, the individual who is being asked to believe two very different things before breakfast – that the world is fair *and* that my hard work isn't getting me as far as others – is going to suffer. They are going to experience mental confusion and conflict which will lead to poorer outcomes for them.

The sweeter spot lies somewhere between a perfect life and a really harsh one – perhaps somewhere 'good enough'. A life which contains goals and ambitions supported by a framework of good advice, realistic appraisal of talent and skillset, hard work, tolerance of failure, flexibility around changes of circumstance, hard work, resilience, hard work ... and, above all, good relationships, interest in the wider world and active engagement with it. You get my drift?

Maybe we *can* change the world, but perhaps we can do that best by first making it mentally healthier. As individuals, we all have a huge part to play in that production, especially at a time when every day brings a new headline telling us that this or that is the answer to all

22   Thomas Curran and Andrew P. Hill, Perfectionism is increasing over time: a meta-analysis of birth cohort differences from 1989 to 2016, *Psychological Bulletin* 145(4) (2017): 410–429.

23   Graham Greene, *The Heart of the Matter* (London: Vintage, 2004 [1948]), p. 50.

24   Tom Whipple, Why belief in a fair world kills poor children's hopes and dreams, *The Times* (20 June 2017).

of life's problems, swiftly followed by a headline telling us the exact opposite. As parents and educators, we can help children to understand that there is usually a healthy middle ground to be found – if we look for it.

Parenting Goldilocks (or hitting the sweet spot)

- You love your child, of course, and your child is perfect (to you), but too much praise and admiration can lead to an inflated sense of entitlement and importance which can be demotivating.[25] 'If I'm so great, why bother doing any more?' It's a myth that it's bad for children to feel shame. A study from Northern Ireland showed that experiencing regret improves decision-making, so preventing children from experiencing regret could actually be bad for them.[26] Regret allows a child to realise that with different decisions there are different outcomes, and so they have both choice (flexibility) and agency. Overall, allowing a child to feel less than perfect can be good for their development – provided they also learn how they can improve the situation.

- Help children to realise that it may be a whole lot easier to adapt themselves to circumstances, rather than expect the world (of seven billion others) to adapt to them. This can be demonstrated on the beach when they are small: hold up one grain of sand and let their imaginations run with the idea of what it must do to affect all the others.

- Talk to children about other people and possibilities ('If we do that then X will/won't be able to …'), so they understand that complexity and perspective is involved in decision-making. It's not all about 'me'. Help children to learn this in greater depth, as well as become open-minded to other ideas, by having round-the-table debates at meal times (family meals around a table are really good for children's development) when they can explore and listen to varying points of view. Intergenerational mealtimes are valuable, too.

---

25 Possibly lowering children's dopamine levels and so their general wellbeing.
26 Eimear O'Connor, Teresa McCormack and Aidan Feeney, Do children who experience regret make better decisions? A developmental study of the behavioral consequences of regret, *Child Development* 85(5) (2014): 1995–2010.

- Although happiness is great, life can't always be happy for everyone, so help children to accept less than perfect times with patience and grace. Model acceptance for them in your own behaviour.

- Likewise, although high ambition is also great, not everyone is going to reach the stars. Help children to moderate their expectations to fit their personal reality (without dumping down on them). Encourage them to explore alternative options to those set in stone by an often unrealistic and prejudiced society (perhaps an apprenticeship rather than a degree), and talk to them about the realities of work, the challenges of combining multiple roles and so on. Take them to work with you and let them experience 'grown-up life'. Better informed is better prepared.

- Part of being prepared is knowing what is actually out there. Death, illness and so on are difficult subjects to talk about, but if children are overly protected they can end up seeing them as nightmare monsters. If a pet has 'run away' or grandma 'has gone to visit family in Australia', how will children ever come to terms with dying, and – once they know the truth – how will they ever trust you again? Age-appropriate acknowledgement that grandma will not be coming back is ultimately better for them, if not sweeter for adults to communicate.

- There is a sweet spot between hypersensitivity and brutal challenge; it's called robustness (the close cousin of resilience). Parents who prevent children from experiencing difficult emotions or from taking risks tend to leave them more at risk of vulnerability in the face of difficult events. They won't learn their own limits or capabilities and won't develop strategies for dealing with hot stimuli like fear, anxiety and even thrills. Robust children have opportunities to test their own coping skills – when they walk to the shops alone, when they deal with a child who is being less than kind (I'm not talking bullying here), when they have to manage their spending money without being bailed out and so on – again, in age-appropriate ways.

- Parents are sometimes most challenged by how to manage their own emotional dramas (such as divorce) without harming their children. To come out of a bad situation with the best outcome in the circumstances means asking whose emotions are driving parental behaviour – their own feelings about either the situation or their partner or their child's current and future feelings? Very rarely is any individual completely right in such situations, so the sweetest spot in a not very sweet world is the one that allows the prefrontal cortex to dominate the amygdala. Nobody said it was easy, but at least children can take away something positive.

- This is really a catch-all for adults in general: gender politics often begin in the home and are not always a good model for children's acceptance that there can be different ways of dealing with emotions. For example, it has become a given that sharing emotional matters and digging deeply into your inner distress, or even delight, is the most authentic way to relate to those with whom you wish to be close. However, the reality is that forcing people – often males – to access their 'inner selves' is often felt as bullying rather than supportive. A middle ground should be less prescriptive, and allow that men may experience and do some things differently from women, and vice versa – *but* there is nothing sinister in the difference. When evolutionary biologist Robin Dunbar from Oxford University studied how friendships survived transitional periods in life, he found a very clear pattern: men kept relationships going longer and felt more supported by simply having a few beers with their mates – boys had to keep on doing and going to things together. In contrast, girls had to make real efforts to stay in conversational contact with one another.[27] Some people, of either gender, like to do both – and that is what the sweet middle ground is all about.

Educating Goldilocks (or hitting the sweet spot)

- On the matter of gender difference, we might as well look into another possible (educational) misperception: young girls are better at reading than young boys, which gives them an early years advantage. In reality girls tend to do better in tests, but this may be down to the way reading is tested. Most tests ask

---

27 Tom Whipple, Having a few beers is the best way to maintain male friendships, *The Times* (20 February 2017). When I worked as a college lecturer I discovered this for myself. Some girls in a class were giving the boys a hard time for being 'emotionally illiterate', so I checked with the boys to see if they experienced times of close emotional bonding with their friends. The outcome was unanimous: they did so in the pub. The girls were reluctantly convinced but remained unimpressed.

children to draw out meaning from long continuous pieces of writing, which girls are usually more proficient at than boys (although Victorian males – Dickens, Thackeray, Trollope – were clearly no slouches in this respect). If tests used shorter pieces and/or graphs, charts or adverts, so the argument goes, then the boys would be coming out at least as well. Our current system may well be creating a situation in which belief makes reality, and boys end up thinking of themselves as non-readers. Sweet spot? A variety of texts.

● We also need a balance between brain and body, academic and physical learning. We now know that the two are very much interconnected (forget Descartes), so children should learn both about the ways their bodies influence their brains in physics, chemistry, biology, cookery, psychology and so on *and* take part in physical exercise. Adults with depression are known to have smaller hippocampi, and involvement in team sports has been shown to increase hippocampal size. This applies to children as well as adults, and boys aged from 9 to 11 involved in team sports in particular showed reduced rates of depression compared with their peers. Dr Cynthia LaBella of the American Academy of Pediatrics Council on Sports Medicine and Fitness, who was involved in the research, said that apart from offering brain-healthy aerobic activity, team sports also provide social networks, a sense of purpose, belonging and achievement.[28] Brains and bodies in balance.

● Another form of balance that is good for young people is between acquiring a lot of knowledge (data banks which will provide that all-important cognitive reserve) *and* opinion and enquiry. When teaching, I found that many foreign students, rather embarrassingly, knew more about English history and literature than my own dear students, but they were very often critical of their own relative lack of critical skills. This relies on openness to alternative ideas and challenges to orthodoxy (the UK system is actually quite good at this). At the same time, young people need to be open to counter-critiquing, so opinions should also be founded on a bank of established knowledge. In this way you get a win-win: mental capital that keeps brains going and flexibility of attitude to support mental health.

---

28 Lisa Gorham, Terry Jernigan, Jim Hudziak and Deanna Barch, Involvement in sports, hippocampal volume, and depressive symptoms in children, *Biological Psychiatry: Cognitive Neuroscience and Neuroimaging* 4(5) (2019): 484–492.

- A spin-off from the previous point is Gradgrind vs. the student activist, or dry-as-dust-rationality vs. passion, both of which can be equally narrow. The middle ground? Debate. Simple.

- The *Times* recently reported that grammar schools were not the 'key to happiness' and that children were equally content at selective and grammar schools, although students at selective schools had higher expectations of staying on and going to university.[29] However, their sister paper, the *Sunday Times*, has previously said that 'gromp' schools, which combine being comprehensive with behaving like a grammar school – strict discipline, uniforms, longer days, competitive sports and tougher subject choices, including Latin – were the most successful.[30] As individual student behaviour is a reliable indicator of their future success and wellbeing in life, regardless of IQ or many other apparent predictors, it seems that schools which instil discipline are not only getting the results but also doing young people a brain favour, which is obvious once you know that self-discipline is associated with so many brain benefits.[31] Brain health is linked to good behaviour in school – if not causally, then by association – suggesting that rather than focusing on creating happiness in schools, hoping that achievement will be a desirable by-product, we should be focusing on better behaviour, knowing that at least success will be an outcome.

- Arts vs. sciences. Why are we so fixated on students taking one path or the other? It's yet another way to divide society. A wider and more inclusive perspective would be better – cross-fertilisation, showing how science and art come together to make culture, and how psychology, neuroscience, biology, history and linguistics (at the very least) may all be needed to understand a text or a philosophy. This would bring nuance to learning and help to reduce narrow silo thinking. Our neural networks would be stimulated to make sense of more things and we would all be more balanced. This is where individual teachers can make a real difference – by keeping their own minds open to wide-ranging lifelong learning and by trying to educate in that way as much as possible.

---

29 Nicola Woolcock, Grammars are not key to happiness, parents told, *The Times* (1 March 2019).

30 Sian Griffiths, 'Gromp' schools romp to top of class, *Sunday Times* (20 August 2017).

31 And wholly in line with Walter Mischel's seminal work on marshmallows.

Another question of almost equal interest to me is: why should everything be made relevant to a child's current experience? Isn't that the very opposite of learning? From Shakespeare to historical events, it seems that the subjective approach to learning is considered to be more valuable, more 'authentic' and better at engaging students – not to mention more fun. But isn't this just another outcome of the I, myself and me thinking which is also found in our general cultural bias towards confessional outpourings in journalism, fiction, social media and so-called reality TV?

The focus on relatable personal or domestic topics and modules – at the expense of more objective, chronological teaching – means taking thematic chunks of history, looking at them from an often contemporary viewpoint, with little attempt to link them or analyse how they came about or influenced what followed, and so failing to help students develop overview, context or an understanding of cause and effect.[32] By making everything 'relevant' – often with modern-dress costume, updated language and superimposed culturally 'woke' reinterpretations – are we telling children that there is nothing to be learned from the past? That *my* experience is what matters and that *now* is superior to then? That children don't need to take the trouble to use their imaginations to inhabit a different world and mindset, and, in effect, that life will not involve them going out to visit new ground because everything will come to them in the sanctity of their homes?

Better for young people's mental health, as well as their imaginations, to ask them to step out of their own and put themselves into another person's shoes – shoes walked in at other times, over different, mostly rockier ground and in other countries (to borrow from L. P. Hartley's metaphor that 'the past is a foreign country'). In this way they will understand that there are only relative certainties, that absolutism isn't always good for you (there is often another side to a story) and that it's

---

32 But much to generate an unhealthy sense of superior difference, and especially so if accompanied by questions such as, 'How would you have felt if, after a long working day in a steamy environment, you had to sleep on the floor of Hampton Court's kitchens?' Often asked without any explanation of how feelings derive from cultural expectations and therefore that sixteenth-century thought processes and feelings would have been very different from our own. The question is more or less totally irrelevant educationally – but it does a lot to sugar-coat self-importance.

best to keep an open mind about some things – including the historical accuracy of what they see in the media.

We live in a time of divisions, opposing rights and entitlements. If we can't all have things the way we want them to be (and how could that ever be possible?), then it seems obvious that we do our children the best of favours by helping them to understand the benefits of balance, of the middle ground, of the sweet spot between idealism and pure unrelenting pragmatism. That is where the brain is at its most comfortable.

Chapter 9

'I'dentity

'Who am I?' is one of the most enduring – and most unanswerable – questions in the world. Shakespeare, who knew a bit about human obsessions, cleverly began the best-known play in the world with these words:

Barnardo: Who's there?

Francisco: Nay, answer me. Stand and unfold yourself.

He then went on to fix on the questions of what it takes to be a man (or a woman for that matter – he was the original gender-fluid writer) and how we might work out who we really are in this world. His world, in case anyone thinks Shakespeare, or *Hamlet*, is irrelevant if it's not updated, was a world that should still be familiar to us. It was/is one in which families are troublesome and can't understand their children, cultural values are confused, love is conflicted, and the pressure and expectation to conform are placed on you by everything and everyone, from the state to your (supposed) best friends. Oh, and something out there is watching your every move. Yes, it really is!

Since the start of the seventeenth century and our first meeting with the oh-so conflicted Hamlet, it seems that we haven't stopped searching for 'I'. We try to find ourselves through our clothes, our homes, our hair and our tribes – not to mention our beliefs. And yet we still don't know for sure that there is something that could reasonably be called 'I' out there – or, indeed, in there.

Einstein, another big beast in the global brain stakes, said: 'A human being … experiences himself, his thoughts and feelings as something separate from the rest – a kind of optical delusion of his consciousness. The striving to free oneself from this delusion is the one issue of true religion. Not to nourish the delusion but to try to overcome it is the way to reach the attainable measure of peace of mind.'[1] The Buddhist concept of *anatta*, or non-self, also teaches that the idea of a central self is an illusion – one which is at the heart of much human unhappiness.

So, where does that leave us?

Well, perhaps at the mercy of a biological trickster or mischief-maker, which is the take of a number of scientists who have suggested that everything we think we have decided to do is in fact the product of *pre-conscious* brain behaviour, and that what the trickster does is to add intention and meaning into the mix. The reason for this, according to the theory, is to help us create a solid vehicle for thoughts, which we are then able to pass on to others via gesture or language, so achieving the evolutionary or survival advantage that comes with being part of a wider social group. There is a whole lot of interesting work around this, but we're not really here to talk heavy-consciousness science, just what makes us 'us'.

And one thing that makes humans unique among animals (nearly – some capuchin monkeys do funny things with bananas) is the ability to deceive others or to fake it (again, there is an evolutionary advantage to doing this). This is where that trickster comes in again, because the first person we deceive most often is the first person: 'I'. Not only do we tell ourselves that we meant to do things that we actually had no control over, but we also fabricate a whole lot of things that we both hold dear and like to think of as being the indestructible foundation stones of I, myself and me.

For example, our perception of our own talents, morality and intellect is likely to be considerably distorted by what is known as 'illusory superiority', unless we are clinically depressed. We're not so hot at singing, driving, telling the truth, helping the disadvantaged or predicting exam results accurately as we might fondly imagine.[2]

More worryingly, we are also capable of fabricating memories – and memories, plus the brain regions that are involved in creating them, turn out to play a huge role in who we are – which can lead to all

---

1   Albert Einstein, Letter to Robert S. Marcus (12 February 1950), in Alice Calaprice (ed.), *The New Quotable Einstein* (Princeton, NJ: Princeton University Press, 2005). This has curious parallels to my central idea in *The Significance Delusion*.

2   'You are an exceptionally gifted person that others do not recognise' is one of the most delusion-like beliefs in the UK.

kinds of problems. The high priestess of research in this field is American psychologist Elizabeth Loftus. Not only has she demonstrated how easy it is to get someone to 'remember' that a car involved in a crash was travelling much faster than it really was, simply by adding emotionally charged words into questions about the crash, but she has also shown that it is possible to make up complete chunks of personal history.[3]

She gives examples of people having 'remembered' voting in elections (when they haven't), becoming lost in shopping malls (that didn't exist), fighting in wars (when they weren't in the army) and perhaps worst of all, being sexually abused as children (when no such thing happened). It is well worth getting to know her work on false memory syndrome, as this misremembering is technically known. It shows us that we shouldn't rely too heavily on what people say they remember (or perhaps on self-evaluation of any kind), no matter how culturally and politically convenient it may be to do so.[4]

With the question of identity back in the hot seat, this shows us that we shouldn't always trust the stories we've been telling ourselves about ourselves.

Am I really who I think I am?

Given that there now appears to be a sloppy quagmire where we thought there was a solid foundation of rock, what does our sense of self, our identity, depend on?

When people suffer brain damage they often lose their sense of who they were, but their families and friends may stubbornly reject the idea that they are no longer 'themselves' (unless, apparently, brain damage has caused them to become dishonest – and then people seem much happier to accept there has been a far-reaching change). When brain-damaged people themselves can't recognise the change and have no insight into their own condition it is called anosognosia, but with families and friends who are unwilling to recognise what is different, it's perhaps more a case of a willing delusion around

---

3   Clare Wilson, Memory special: can you trust your memories?, *New Scientist* (27 October 2018). Available at: https://www.newscientist.com/article/mg24032010-700-memory-special-can-you-trust-your-memories.

4   It seems that social media users who make their lives more interesting than they really are will also be laying down false memories. How will social history be catalogued in the future – as fact or fiction?

identity.[5] Most of the time they simply don't want to look at the accumulation of evidence; they prefer to remember the memory of the person before the brain damage and make that 'reality'.

Memory also seems to play a huge part in our belief that we have a central self. Parts of the brain that help to create autobiographical memories – that is, memories of episodes and events from our own past experience – are probably most strongly linked to our sense of self: the belief that we have one unchanging identity.[6] The areas involved include the anterior cingulate cortex and the hippocampus, and evidence shows that damage to these areas does indeed impact on a person's sense of self.

If you are a fan of the TV series *Sherlock*, you will know that when Sherlock is trying to retrieve a piece of information he goes into what he calls his 'mind palace', which is essentially a process of navigation through the passages of his memory. The hippocampus is associated with both memory and navigation, which explains why black cab drivers are often also whizzes at quizzes. It might also explain why one of the first indications of many forms of dementia is getting lost 'in space' (or not finding your way when out and about). One of the saddest features of dementia is that very often, especially in the early stages, people can sense their own sense of self slipping away and make desperate attempts to grasp at it before it's too late.

But what are they reaching out for, if not an illusion? A box of memories that may or may not be constructed of real events? An image that is increasingly being created with social media in mind? A constructed persona that has to be acceptable to family and friends?

It was probably a lot easier to feel confident about identity in the past (however illusory in truth), before the age of radio, TV, telephones and cinema, not to mention social media, the internet, rolling news and all the other developments of our 'civilised society'. These have brought us more possibilities – more options and

---

5   Some of the saddest of these cases involve parents of very brain-damaged children, some of whom have been born without any brain matter to speak of. Parents will insist that he or she is 'still in there', or believe there is a personality of sorts with a fighting spirit who will win through.

6   Unsurprisingly, some forms of deception use the same neural pathways, which seems to suggest that a sense of self is, at heart, a lie.

choices[7] – and an infinity of infinitely perfectible alternatives of who and what we are.

Recent generations, such as the baby boomers, have been able to enjoy certainties like progression through school-job-family or school-university-career-family, and relative stability in terms of societal and social norms. But how can today's young people feel as confident of their place and identity when all around them is in a state of rapid change? It's enough to make even Hamlet scratch his head. But his creator had the answer: easy-peasy, you turn to the world of make-believe. When you don't know who you are, when nothing is fixed and everything is a choice, you can select stories, roles, costumes, props and scripts to help you sell a chosen version of yourself to your audience.

When your performance goes well the applause can be deafening, so you can believe in the audience's belief and that feels fabulous. You *are* that person, for a time, and the more you see pictures of you in that role, with that make-up, striking those poses, speaking those lines, the more you believe that *is* your reality. And those pictures become your memories of who you are: 'That's my history.' Unless, or until, you don't get the hoped for positive feedback. Then, either your audience is wrong or the script is wrong, or you are wrong. So, you either fall apart or try on another identity for size. Why not?

It's not for nothing that when we think about identity we talk about 'losing ourselves', 'finding ourselves', 'voyages of self-discovery' and the rest. These are all expressions connected with place, journeying and locations, and these in turn are connected with the hippocampus – that part of the brain which 'does' memory and navigation. It's also surely not surprising then that when individuals identify with other people – whether real ones or dramatic creations – with their situations, experiences, pain and so on, or identify with causes and beliefs, they are very often looking for that place where they feel they can belong. It's similar to a homecoming, and we often hear someone say, 'I felt like I'd come home', when they make such connections.

It may all be brain behaviour, but like so much other brain behaviour it can feel very sweet. Being without a place where you feel you belong can taste very sour, so there is nothing at all odd about

---

7   Choice can be a very mixed blessing. Yes, it brings options, but it also can be very destabilising, especially to a vulnerable brain: 'Which way should I go, this way or that or that?' The end result is often stasis.

wanting to find a sense of self through a sense of belonging in what appears to be a stable world. It's only when someone has previously been very lost and when the playacting becomes too experimental, too dangerous or too damaging that things start to get worrying.

The less stable a person's early environment and experiences, the more likely they are to turn to the clamour (and glamour) of experimentation and of risky productions and damaging roles to big up their sense of self. In other words, the more likely they are to take on identities that are full of character to get big reactions from others that bring the corroborating feedback that has been missing from their life.

It's one thing to put on the clothes and the voice of a character to win approval, but what happens when the role takes a darker turn and other's reactions confirm a negative, conflicted or unhealthy self-image? Does that drive or follow mental health difficulties?

What follows may be controversial, but all possibilities should be explored if we want to improve young people's mental health. (Having a closed mind to alternative ways of thinking is a risk factor for mental health problems in itself.) Responding to my views on transitioning children or eating disorders in a rigid way might feel righteous and good, but can you be sure that you are not overdosing on some very dark chocolate indeed?

In at the deep end, then. What is the nature of the relationship between the following issues with identity and mental health? Is it chicken or egg?

- Transitioning children. These are young people, sometimes very young pre-teens, who believe they are in wrongly gendered bodies and want hormonal and other treatment to change their sex. Janice Turner of *The Times* courted criticism by writing about this in 2018.[8] She cited the work of an American researcher, Lisa Littman of Brown University, who had found that (a) the majority of cases of trans teens she had looked into involved youngsters with very troubled histories, including diagnosed mental health problems, and (b) two significant factors were involved in their stories: 'binge-consumption' of online trans forums and peer contagion – what used to be known as group hysteria. More recently, even professionals

---

8   Janice Turner, Trans teenagers have become an experiment, *The Times* (18 August 2018).

working in the field have questioned the validity of treatment being carried out on children. Psychoanalyst Dr Marcus Evans has said: 'There is pressure from the child ..., there is pressure from the family and the peer group and from the pro-trans lobbies – and all of this puts pressure on the clinician who may want to help the individual to resolve their distressed state by going along with a quick solution.'[9]

I think this fits very well with what I've been saying: deciding to change your identity by metamorphosing into something you were not born as (whatever you may think about the 'truth' of your original categorisation) is not only extreme experimentation and medically speaking most certainly risky, but it is also one of the oldest examples of identity role play in literature. (Note: Children who self-identify as lesbian, gay or bisexual also have much higher than average levels of mental health problems.[10])

◦ Eating disorders are clearly mental health problems in their own right, and too complex to attempt to explain in detail here, but I do want to mention the language people sometimes use to identify with their eating disorder. They will often say 'my anorexia' or 'my bulimia', which strikes me as a curiously possessive way to describe something that might kill you. It would seem preferable to talk about an eating disorder in a way that allows separation from it without loss: if it's part of you (however unhealthy a part), then ridding yourself of it implies harm to some element of your identity. An alternative might be: 'I have a condition called anorexia, and ...' which suggests a set of factors, not an identity. But, might the creation of an identity be part of its function? A big question.

◦ Cults of melancholia have existed throughout history. States of despair and misery can make a person seem romantic and interesting; it was certainly part of the attraction in the sixteenth century.[11] Suicide can still come out of the blue – even

---

9   Laurel Ives, NHS child gender reassignment 'too quick', *BBC News* (25 February 2019). Available at: https://www.bbc.co.uk/news/health-47359692. See also Deborah Cohen and Hannah Barnes, Transgender treatment: puberty blockers study under investigation, *BBC News* (22 July 2019). Available at: https://www.bbc.co.uk/news/health-49036145.

10 See, for example, Stephen Russell and Jessica Fish, Mental health in gay, bisexual, and transgender youth, *Annual Review of Clinical Psychology* 12(1) (2016): 465–487.

11 Aristocratic young men are depicted leaning moodily and interestingly against trees in Nicholas Hilliard's miniatures.

following claims of extreme happiness – and may sometimes follow the high-profile deaths of public figures such as Robin Williams and Kurt Cobain. This is known as the copycat effect – for example, after Marilyn Monroe killed herself there was a 10–12% rise in the number of suicides.[12] Girls especially seem to identify with the troubled lives of their favourite celebrities, but mass media reporting, particularly of the details of suicide methods, has been implicated as a precipitating factor in people's decisions to take their own life. It has been suggested that those killing themselves in this way have so confused their identity with their idol's that they have a limited ability to understand the implications of their actions on themselves. Even, perhaps, imagining their 'normal' selves as audience members somehow watching their own tragic performance. This kind of death may be the ultimate delusional expression of empathy; the copycat has totally fused their identity with the other.

● Acquiring status through posing as a victim is more common than most people imagine, although it has hit the news headlines recently in the terrible story of 'Nick', committed paedophile and so-called victim of several well-known politicians and public figures.[13] It remains unclear whether he consciously accused others to save himself from being outed or whether it was a knee-jerk self-defence mechanism. I have listened to many similar sob stories, some of staggering complexity and depravity, told by people who seemed to be convinced that what they were claiming was true, while obviously fabricating the lot. What such 'victims' appear to be after is the moist-eyed applause of an audience and a vicarious confession in which they are absolved of the imaginary aggressor's acts.[14]

● Many types of victim identity give shape into formless lives. People who repeatedly go into situations or relationships that leave them damaged in some way should at least raise the

12 See Amy Ellis Nutt, Robin Williams's suicide was followed by a sharp rise in 'copycat' deaths, *Washington Post* (7 February 2018). Available at: https://www.washingtonpost.com/news/to-your-health/wp/2018/02/07/robin-williamss-suicide-was-followed-by-a-sharp-rise-in-copycat-deaths.

13 See https://www.telegraph.co.uk/news/2019/05/15/nick-set-fake-email-back-story-murderous-westminster-vip-paedophile/.

14 I dealt with one sex offender who in a feebly self-pitying way wanted to know if codeine could be blamed for 'making' him do 'silly things'. His crimes: repeated rape of his own daughter.

question, 'What am I getting out of this?' or perhaps, 'Who am I getting out of this?' It could be an identity that strangely works for them – whatever the cost.

● Body image is possibly the stand-out problem of the day, with much talk of selfies impacting on body confidence and the exposure – and even shaming – in social media of anyone who doesn't conform to a particular (artificial and plasticised) notion of beauty. And it's not just girls; boys are now apparently almost as fixated on appearance as girls. The question of whether or not a problem that is shared by such a huge percentage of youngsters can be classified as a mental health disorder is probably one for the whole of society, but let's take a look at it in relation to identity.

Am I a Strongman, or a strong man? A Beauty, or a beautiful woman? A Fashion Icon, or a fashionable person? There is a big difference between thinking of yourself as a Thing (however positive that Thing is), and thinking of yourself as a person with certain attributes. Modern life, with all its advertising and marketing of products to make us physically perfect (or physically sick, if you're of a cynical turn), its distorting mirror of selfie culture[15] and the callous, disconnected, impersonal but targeted cruelty of social media, is perfectly calculated to leave anyone without a sturdy sense of self in a state of self-doubt and self-disgust. And self-disgust is not a good identity to have.

So who are you? Who am I? What is identity? It seems that identity is likely to be a delusion of sorts, a story we tell ourselves about who we are, but it works to stabilise this bag of bones and brains we call 'me' and give it a structure and shape that can be recognised and related to by other people. Certain styles of upbringing will work better than others to provide the basic framework and ingredients for a consistent and healthy story, but if we haven't had that lucky start we tend to 'borrow' stories we would like to be part of and 'play act' the characters we would like to be. And the more negatively we feel about ourselves, the more conflicted or unhealthy the stories and characters are likely to be.

---

15 Nobody but the selfie taker ever sees themselves like that – a selfie is *always* a distortion.

If you're looking to big up your sense of who you are (despite realising that 'you' is only ever a construct of the trickster inside you, but nevertheless wanting to be that sturdier construct), then don't limit yourself too much. Don't call yourself a runner; say you're a person who enjoys running. Don't be an activist; be a person who likes to be involved in human rights. Don't be an accountant, teacher, mechanic (unless you really, really want to); be a person who is an accountancy professional, teaches, repairs cars or builds aircraft. If too much is invested in one thing, one cause or one assumed identity, you narrow down your possibilities as well as other people's perception of you.

Too narrow an identity can be a straightjacket; but it can also be, like swaddling, a comforter. If a person is too tightly bound up in the clothes they wear, the props they have about them and the image they project, when one thing gets removed the whole bundle may unravel, and mental health can suffer.

In this chapter I have identified a number of issues that may affect young people, in particular, but there are many other possibilities out there. I wouldn't want anyone to feel excluded (especially victims)! Other ways of claiming an identity that can boost your sense of being that little bit special and interesting, and therefore more likely to get audience applause and approval, are as: drunk, addict, sick person, hero(ine), nice person, humane person, forward-thinker, clever clogs, risk-taker, rescuer, saint, self-sacrificer, aesthete, ultra-sensitive person, empathiser, animal lover, passionate person, activist (been there already), savvy person, cynic, hard guy, wise guy, funny guy, couldn't care about any of it sort of guy …

We all need some definition in our lives, especially if we suspect that it is only a kind of mirage in the first place, but being too closely defined by, and identified with, a role, is less evidence of solidity than it is fear of meaninglessness. As Hamlet says, 'What is a man …?' (or woman etc.). But there are things we can do to help secure a young person's confidence in their identity.

Parenting to support a strong enough sense of identity

Whenever I hear that a potential young client is trying to 'find themselves', I expect to see an unhappy and unfulfilled young person come through the door, one whose childhood has been less than perfect, leaving them with a lack of core confidence. The idea that an 'authentic self' exists is a powerful one, but once we accept that there is no such thing as a permanent 'real' self, because everything, even memories, are simply constructs of a sometimes whimsical and variable brain, then we have to look into ways of helping our brains to develop regular enough patterns of activity that it *seems* like there is some regularity and stability.

⬤ Anxiety and depression are major causes of brain instability. A new baby can seem pretty disconnected from all that is going on around them, but *everything* counts as learning for that baby; even carers' own stress and anxiety teach the infant something. The learning is very deep: scientists from the Salk Laboratory of Genetics have shown a connection between styles of caring, whether attuned[16] or neglectful, and genetic changes associated with depression and schizophrenia (perhaps the ultimate loss of self) in offspring. They speculate that neglectful parenting and the changing gene patterns are probably outcomes of stress in mothers.[17] Their research involved mice, but other studies have shown that anxious parenting leaves children at twice the risk of anxiety and depression.[18]

And it's not only the genes at fault: anxious parents expect their children to be anxious. The solution is to try not to read anxiety in your child's expressions and behaviour, and avoid rewarding them for fearful responses – for example, with treats to make them feel better or with extra attention. Anxious parents are often self-absorbed and so less likely to set and enforce appropriate boundaries, and more likely to model anxious behaviour, leaving children feeling insecure. The solution is to seek professional help (preferably before the child is born), which will provide useful techniques and pay dividends. 'Fake it to make it' really can work: playing confident can fire up neural circuits which help you to feel confident. And confident

---

16 Attuned doesn't have to mean physically available 24/7. There is a world of difference between a smothering full-on presence and full-on mothering attention when present.

17 Tracy A. Bedrosian, Carolina Quayle, Nicole Novaresi and Fred H. Gage, Early life experience drives structural variation of neural genomes in mice, *Science* 359(6382) (2018): 1395–1399.

18 Sam Cartwright Hatton, Running in the family: can we help anxious parents to raise confident children? Lecture delivered at Brighton and Sussex Medical School, University of Sussex, 11 April 2018.

parenting results in secure, curious and adventurous babies who will develop a much stronger sense of identity.

- Curiosity in, and exposure to, the outside world results in wider neural connections and wider brain connectivity. Linking multiple brain regions helps to prevent inward focus and promotes flexibility of thought and attitude, resulting in better social skills and connections – both of which are good for what is known as self-esteem and a more solid sense of self. In contrast, brains that rely too heavily on their own internally generated sensations, and don't carry out enough 'reality checks' via the frontal lobes, can experience fragmentation of self – as happens in schizophrenia (schizophrenics often have overactivity in the sensory areas of their brains, but too few connections in the prefrontal areas). Children need to have many and varied experiences and be expected to try new things. Variety and new don't have to mean hyper and expensive; time to be bored and reflect can also amount to experience. It's all about that sweet spot.

- Parents' own sense of identity also has its part to play. An adult whose shaky identity is bolstered by 'playing' carer or feeder can impact on a child's self-image. Munchhausen's syndrome by proxy is currently under review, but I have known several parents who, looking for special status of some kind, have (in the kindest interpretation) become oversensitised to the slightest display of physical infirmity in their child and taken on the role of 'super nurse'. In one case this resulted in a child being kept out of school for months at a time; but she was only ever ill in her mother's company and recovered miraculously when she stayed elsewhere. It will always be hard for that child not to define herself as 'sickly'. All too often, parents feed children old enough to feed themselves, often giving them lots and often; you see them, beaks open like fledglings, barely taking any responsibility for their own eating process. Not only is it an example of how to keep children immature, but it is also a way to define them by their food intake. The solution is for parents to both recognise themselves in their behaviour and very consciously to put the child's future wellbeing before their own emotional needs. Family systems therapy might be helpful in some circumstances.

- In the Instagram and Snapchat age it can be hard to know where family influence ends and peer influence begins, but body image is a complicated matter. The pressure to conform to certain standardised (and idealised) images is causing problems for many young people. Whatever else is going on to make children overly body conscious, the following tale makes for depressing reading; it is an 8-year-old's experience at Brownies:

At the start we met a lady from a professional spa. Then we all had to sit in a line and have people (the other girls) draw lines on our back with their fingers. Then the lady showed us some products which would smooth out wrinkles on our face. She made the older girls put it on. She put it on the 9–10-year-olds! The 7–8-year-olds were taught about face masks. We didn't have to put it on but I thought it was horrible. The mask was supposed to make your skin smooth as well. At the end the older girls had to put cucumber on their face and have their hair wrapped in towels and lay on mats. I thought the whole thing was strange as you don't need face masks or cream until you're about 50! In fact I thought the whole thing was horrible even the badge was bright colours, I wouldn't wear it on my uniform. The whole experience and learning about it so young was pointless. It's silly they teach girls who are so young about that kind of stuff!

The little girl gave up on Brownies after that. I can't imagine that Olave Baden-Powell would have been terribly impressed either. Brownie leaders, although not necessarily parents, are *in loco parentis*, and it would be much more reassuring if they, as well as parents, did more to let young girls know that you can be lovely and valued for more than the sheen on your hair and skin, and that life has a lot more to offer when you're 8 than a spa day. Sometimes children can be a lot wiser than adults.

What really works for body confidence? Paternal care, concern and support has been shown to help with both boys' and girls' body image and self-confidence. The father–son relationship is more important than the mother–son relationship when it comes to eating and obesity; boys with involved fathers are more likely to adopt healthy lifestyles and are less likely to be obese.[19] The father–daughter relationship is more significant than the mother–daughter relationship in matters such as loneliness and coping with adversity; girls with involved fathers feel less lonely as they grow up and are better able to deal with challenges and setbacks.[20] In both cases, the father's relationship with the child appears to be key in setting up a kind of cognitive structure or shape which provides self-confidence – that is, it is good for identity.

As ever, there is a sweet spot, and with parenting it is to be found somewhere between being very involved and supportive and being your child's best friend. According to Barnaby Lenon, former head of Harrow School, fathers who have tried too hard to be 'besties' with their sons can be blamed for a falling off in boys' academic performance and general motivation and behaviour.[21] He's not alone in suspecting that parenting boundaries are getting lost: mothers are also being held to account for wanting to 'get down and dirty' with their daughters or to overshare inappropriate confidences. It can seem to be less a case of wanting to 'bring up' children and more a case of wanting to 'bring down' children – to a level where parents don't feel threatened, left behind or old, but which can leave children at sea in terms of who they should be when their parents are acting like children. Adults should have the confidence in their own identity to give youngsters the space to be different.

Educating to support a strong enough sense of identity

We've looked into the need for wide connectivity between important brain regions, if brains are to develop in ways that support a sense of a continuous self and a strong, connected-up identity. Many of

19 Jess Haines, Sheryl Rifas-Shiman, Nicholas Horton, Ken Kleinman, Katherine Bauer, Kirsten Davison, Kathryn Walton, S. Bryn Austin, Alison Field and Matthew Gillman, Family functioning and quality of parent–adolescent relationship: cross-sectional associations with adolescent weight-related behaviors and weight status, *International Journal of Behavioral Nutrition and Physical Activity* 13, article 68 (2016). DOI: 10.1186/s12966-016-0393-7.

20 Greg Hurst, Why daddy's girls can cope better with setbacks, *The Times* (30 August 2018).

21 Sian Griffiths, Feckless boys blamed on 'best friend' fathers, *Sunday Times* (2 April 2017).

the things that work in education to create those networks have already been covered, but there are other developments in education that could be working in the opposite direction.

● The use of calculators, internet search engines, satnav and other electronic devices, though apparently freeing up brainpower for more creative and useful purposes, in reality seems to be closing down some important brain functions. In this chapter, we have already touched on the connection between black cab drivers and that little brain area shaped like a sea horse, the hippocampus, which is involved in spatial navigation and memory. London taxi drivers have to acquire and pass 'the Knowledge' in order to qualify, which involves knowing their way around all possible routes in London plus associated place and road names and sites of interest. Learning all of this has been shown to increase the size of the hippocampus, and awareness of that effect has helped scientists to understand how necessary the hippocampus is to navigation and memory and how the whole system works.[22] Effectively (as in Sherlock's mind palace), to remember specifics we go on a navigation or journey through our memories until we find what we want – or discover that we're lost in a maze, as the case may be! We map our memories as we map our environment, and as the cab drivers find out, practice makes perfect. So, if we stop practising, the outcome is pretty obvious.

Calculators take the drudgery, and practice, out of making mental maps of the relationships between spaces (numbers, sums, etc.). Internet search engines take the drudgery, and practice, out of making mental maps of relationships between letters, meanings and information in general (dictionaries, encyclopaedias, libraries, etc.). Satnavs take the drudgery, and practice, out of making mental maps of relationships between locations (roads, landscapes, features, etc.).

Various studies indicate that a loss of function in the hippocampus and related memory and navigation areas of the brain may put us at much greater risk of both depression and memory loss later in life. We may be freeing up time, but for what if we end up with less brainpower? And remember that,

---

22 Eleanor A. Maguire, David G. Gadian, Ingrid S. Johnsrude, Catriona D. Good, John Ashburner, Richard S. J. Frackowiak and Christopher D. Frith, Navigation-related structural change in the hippocampi of taxi drivers, *Proceedings of the National Academy of Sciences of the United States of America* 97(8) (2000): 4398–4403.

in the case of identity, to a large extent our identity depends on memory (and navigation). Hmmm. Back to brainpower then, or at least to a mix of electronic and human devices.

- Congruence helps to create a sense of consistent identity, so encouraging youngsters to avoid cognitive dissonance and develop coherent and consistent ideas/philosophies is important. Too often they are swayed by prevailing ideological winds (sometimes through 'passionate' teaching) into attitudes and opinions which aren't truly grounded at a cognitive level – that is, they pick up fashionable attitudes without having any deep understanding. For example, they may say they are concerned about the environment without wanting to give up shopping online for £2 T-shirts or flying off to experience the beaches of Thailand. Philosophy courses in schools can help students to think about thinking itself and encourage a more rigorous examination of behaviour. Well-structured and managed debating societies can encourage students to look into a range of ideas and decide which are the best fit for them individually. Debate can also support young people in standing up for their own substantiated opinions when they go against the flow.

- Classes in literature, biology, media studies, religion and history can all involve detective work into what identity is, how it has been expressed at different times and in different cultures, and how it can be made and unmade by various influences – from families to peer groups to politics to marketing.

- Resilience, at a structural level, is very closely associated with identity – they are both to do with a certain core consistency, so anything that supports resilience should also support a strong sense of identity.

With that in mind, in the following chapter we are going to look at how to build resilience.

Chapter 10

Prehab beats rehab (or how to build resilience)

To listen to many news reports and mental health pundits you would think that the current mental health crisis should be easily solvable – just get everyone talking about their feelings. Job done.

If only it were that easy. If feelings were water, well, it's great not to be frightened of it, but should we simply push in vulnerable people and say, 'Just get on with it. Everyone knows how to swim.' But, of course, they don't. Assuming that people actually want to swim in the first place, they will need to learn the agency and technical control that is involved in swimming, otherwise they will drown. And, believe me, there is nothing particularly pleasant in hearing the drowning cries of people in mental crisis. They are not just talking about their feelings, they are screaming about them.

I won't labour the point, but expressing feelings is not the be-all and end-all of better mental health. As an idea it has its merits, but it also has its downside, which is that it immerses people within themselves, and that is as much the problem as the solution.

As roadside rustic humourists used to say (in the days before satnav), 'Well, if I were going there, I wouldn't be starting here.' It's pretty much what I'm going to say about mental health problems, 'If we are after better mental health, I wouldn't be starting with feelings.' I would be starting with people who have better mental health.[1] This is increasingly looking like an obvious place to start, but that hasn't always been the case. When I started out in the world of addictions and thought that finding out why siblings of addicts weren't addicted would be a good idea, I was seen as a bit of a strange one. However, this now looks like a more useful approach to many researchers.

---

1   This is like prehab. Rather than putting people right after they have gone wrong (as in rehab), prehab is a new direction for medicine, one that aims to build people up so they are going to cope better (and recover better) after surgery. We want to achieve something similar with mental health.

Resilience studies are telling us ever more about how the brain works when it is able to withstand the pressures that tip people over into mental health problems. What I'm going to attempt here is to translate as much of that as possible into real-life processes and actions. Sadly, what there won't be – and this may come as a surprise – is a simple single solution or strategy.[2] This is going to involve a number of different factors.

In one resilience study, participants aged from 90 to 101 had worse physical but better mental health than younger family members aged from 51 to 75.[3] Researchers focused on their personal attributes rather than genetics or other more obviously 'scientific' things, and what they have discovered about these clearly highly resilient people is of great practical interest to all of us. They found that 'the unique features associated with better mental health of this rural population, were positivity, work ethic, stubbornness and a strong bond with family, religion and land'. In addition, they 'care less about what others think' and have 'a need to adapt to changing circumstances'.

So, they have many of the essential ingredients of resilience, or the ability to bounce back from whatever life throws at them. They are well-connected socially, and presumably that means across generations rather than with an identikit peer group. They feel they belong in and to their 'place'. They are firm in their beliefs but still ready to roll with the blows. They are not at the mercy of others' fleeting judgements (i.e. that short-term audience applause and approval). And, perhaps as important as all the rest, they are optimistic in outlook and work very hard.

If we add to those findings other research which has showed that army veterans who serve longer live longer too, and in better health,[4] then what we have is evidence that commitment has a big part to play in general wellbeing, suggesting that the fluid lifestyle of many millennials may not be so much life enhancing as life limiting. This is despite their apparent ability to stay flexible around lifestyle,

---

2   In our instant gratification, high sugar society we want immediate hits, whether of pleasure or of sound-bite level information. Things that work in reality, rather than as a headline, might involve slightly more complexity.

3   Anna Scelzo, Salvatore Di Somma, Paola Antonini, Lori Montross, Nicholas Schork, David Brenner and Dilip Jeste, Mixed-methods quantitative–qualitative study of 29 nonagenarians and centenarians in rural Southern Italy: focus on positive psychological traits, *International Psychogeriatrics* 30(1) (2018): 31–38.

4   Douglas Barrie, Veterans who serve longer live on, *The Scotsman* (20 March 2019).

location, working practices and so on. It seems that flexibility is most useful within an overall framework; without that it begins to look like tumbleweed.

The military life has its fair share of trauma, of course, and nowadays many reported cases of PTSD, but even so there are numerous examples of serving personnel who appear to experience very few mental health problems. Perhaps times and expectations were different (and expectations determine the way we react to events), but some of those who flew in the Battle of Britain recall a time that was far from terrible. One pilot interviewed in 2015 said, 'strangely enough it was a good life. I enjoyed it.' And another, 'It was a matter of luck if you survived or not. But at the end of it all, it was the happiest time of my life, though I lost a lot of good friends.'[5] This wasn't merely a case of 'misremembering' the past, either. Much more recently, veterans of the Afghan campaign have described the thrill of being in the thick of combat and of the huge highs that come with the heady mixture of comradeship and adrenaline.

Feeling really alive isn't only about having fun, or at least having fun is not only about being safe. Why else extreme sports? It's all down to that interesting hormone dopamine again which, as we know, makes life meaningful, if not necessarily moral. So, making meaning, even in a crisis, should help with resilience, and it turns out it probably does.

When East German Gilbert Furian was arrested by the Stasi, held in a miserable cell and subjected to psychological torture, rather than give in to his first inclination to break down he took charge of himself and his emotions (that prefrontal goddess again): 'I thought of it as an abstract process, like in a Kafka novel. I said to myself, "You are a character, you do what you're told."'[6] He was treating himself as both second and third person (see page 38) and adding a shape and context to his story.

The article in which Furian is mentioned, which looks at the work of Europe's first resilience research centre, goes on to discuss other examples of coping in the face of adversity, and quotes a researcher

---

5   Graham Keeley, War hero, 100, given a fitting birthday treat, *The Times* (20 September 2018).

6   Quoted in Tony Andrews, 'I put myself in standby mode': what makes a survivor?, *The Guardian* (7 January 2017). Available at: https://www.theguardian.com/society/2017/jan/07/put-myself-standby-mode-what-makes-a-survivor.

who agrees that 'we need to be able to create a narrative out of capricious events'. In other words, we need to make meaning out of them. One of the final findings cited supports another theme of this book: 'suppressing emotions has long been thought to be detrimental to recovery [i.e. after a traumatic event]. But research has found that, directly after a trauma, it can be helpful to suppress the memories for a time in order simply to get on with daily life.' Or with routine, another dull but necessary feature of most people's lives. It's that necessary structure or framework again.

Many of the things we have been told are essential to good mental health are challenged by much of what I have written about in this book. I'm effectively saying that a lot of the advice we've been given should be binned. But there is another regular headline-grabber that I haven't said a lot about yet, which I'm also about to demote a bit, and that is stress itself.

It is a given that stress is bad for us; so bad, in fact, that it has become a code word for bad. 'I'm *soooo* stressed' doesn't need any suggestion of cause or cure. It is a declaration of a negative state, pure and simple (not to mention a universal excuse for all sorts of unwanted behaviour). It almost doesn't matter how it has come to take on the role of universal baddie, a kind of Jaws or Lord Voldemort of the mental state. What matters is that it has been traduced, misrepresented and vilified. The baddie must be understood and seen for what it really is, which, if not a warm, cuddly, thoroughly likeable and sympathetic character, is at least a more complex one, which is both a thoroughly acceptable and necessary part of the human story.

Stress has a huge part to play in resilience (see footnote 5 on page 80). Not only does supported and sympathetic exposure to stress and stressors at an early age help a child to develop resilience, but it also helps children to realise that the world is not a completely flat and smooth plateau. It has lots of bumpy bits, too, some of which may tip them into quite deep ravines.[7] It's only when other people, who have influence over a child's mental state, show anxiety and fear around stress that it becomes a 'bad thing' in its own right. Learning to be on frenemy terms with stress is essential to resilience.

Pain is very much like stress, in that it also gets a bad press, but like stress it is horribly misrepresented. Pain is necessary; without it we

---

7   For pure and absolute infant resilience in the face of such challenge, take a look at the 'Emperor' episode, set in Antarctica, from series 1 of BBC One's *Dynasties*.

would end up cut, bruised, bland and possibly even stupid. Some recent evidence has shown that a rather shy and retiring part of the brain, the insular cortex, is involved in our experience of pain.[8] It seems likely that it is on better terms with the hot-hatch amygdala than was initially realised, and probably sends it little coded messages telling it to yell and scream as appropriate (according to upbringing) whenever it feels the body being assaulted (brain regions can be very proprietorial about the body). This is how we essentially learn to avoid future harmful situations, which is known as threat learning.[9]

Processed sensibly, the connections between situation, pain, learning and avoidance are of immense importance to the survival of the species. But, as with stress, if the possibility of pain is avoided at all costs, then experience will be kept to a very smooth and inoffensive baseline and fewer life lessons will be learned.

In the cases of both pain and stress, acceptable levels of exposure are better for the development of resilience than avoidance. Exposure suggests engagement, connection, even friction, and taking the rough with the smooth – in general, mixing it up. This doesn't sit well with a culture that also believes in perfectibility and extreme individual Rights. Once again, it has become sweeter to enjoy the fudge of ease and indulgence than to digest the grittier reality of effort and occasional conflict.

This brings me on to the question of cross-fertilisation. Without that wider mix of generational influences, alternative experiences and tastes, how can anyone develop the resilience I've been describing? Even the elderly Italians who were involved in the resilience studies, though geographically isolated, were involved in discussions across the generations. They had what is now called a 'positive mental outlook' and were flexible about change (after all, they had grown up in a time of global upheaval that we can hardly comprehend today). All in all, they were familiar with both friction and the need to adapt.

---

8   Emmanuelle Berret, Michael Kintscher, Shriya Palchaudhuri, Wei Tang, Denys Osypenko, Olexiy Kochubey and Ralf Schneggenburger, Insular cortex processes aversive somatosensory information and is crucial for threat learning, *Science* 364(6443) (2019): eaaw0474.

9   The insular cortex is also involved in addiction, particularly to nicotine. The connection appears to be: no insular cortex, no smoking – make of that what you will.

I don't blame the kids who are stuck with a samey diet of sugary self-indulgence, having had very little exposure to the roughage of challenge. But I do blame an older generation who, for the sake of their own emotional sweet tooth, have refused children the opportunity to test themselves or take risks with their thought processes. Presumably they don't want to be thought of as adult-centric, and believe that giving youngsters what feels right for them or what they are asking for (on a minute-by-minute basis) must be best for them – almost on the Rousseau-esque principle that natural inclinations are healthy ones. Hmmm, really?

According to a study carried out by the University of Warwick, Britain's happiest year in recent times was 1957.[10] They acknowledge that the conditions would now be seen as poverty-stricken and primitive, but concluded that people, having been through terrible historical events, were probably reasonably thankful for what they had, more realistic in their expectations of what happiness amounted to and felt more connected to others. People did more, too. They had to: adults walked everywhere and children's games were much more physical, energetic and tactile. Meccano, which developed manual dexterity, spatial awareness and understanding of mechanical properties and relationships, was a huge favourite (of many girls as well as boys).[11]

In another study, the University of Essex has concluded that children are getting physically weaker.[12] They have grown taller and heavier but lost their strength and fitness. This is a big worry because strength and fitness are not only essential for long-term physical health but also for mental health – a fact which is being understood a bit too late in the day to stop the sale of half the nation's school playing fields.

Children once had no alternative but to walk to school, usually on their own or in groups. This led to two things: free-form play, which involved games (often self-invented), trees, green spaces and so on;

10 Rosemary Bennett, We've never had it so good: 1957 was the happiest year, *The Times* (24 January 2017).

11 According to one professor of surgery, today's students, who are used to so much screen time, are losing the necessary dexterity to become good surgeons. See Kat Lay, New surgeons 'lack dexterity after too much screen-time', *The Times* (31 October 2018). His point is debatable – but that's just it, we should explore the counterarguments.

12 BBC News, Fall in strength and fitness of 10-year-olds, study shows (26 September 2018). Available at: https://www.bbc.co.uk/news/health-45651719.

and hierarchies and negotiations, not always friendly ones, but that was where the creative friction came in.[13] For boys (be still, my thundering heart – can I say this?), quick resolution of conflict is often preferable to long-drawn-out investigations of inner cause and consequence. Experiences like these, before the school run was invented, meant that youngsters saw themselves in many ways, as much more autonomous than they do now.

Being autonomous and having or taking responsibility are closely connected – both involve feeling proactive, which is where much of modern life fails young people. Too often they are simply not allowed to feel as if they are 'stakeholders' in their households or families. A stakeholder has an invested concern in a business, which suggests both that they contribute meaningful and necessary money or effort and that they have an equal interest in how well the enterprise runs. Children who worked in family businesses could experience this (as they still do in much of the Third World), and children who are carers probably feel this much more than is healthy (as ever this is about the sweet spot), but how many other young people do today?

The reality is that children are treated more like special pets in many families. And, heaven knows, pets are treated badly enough, what with all the treats, obesity and lack of purposeful activity. Don't our children deserve better than to be petted, but left with the sense that their value is little more than decorative, especially when feeling valued for your involvement and contribution is likely to give you a far greater sense of connectedness and wellbeing?

Baroness Brady, of *The Apprentice* fame, suggests that children need to volunteer and work, and become known as 'Generation Citizen' rather than 'Generation Snowflake'.[14] Although I wholeheartedly agree with her,[15] I wouldn't put the whole responsibility onto children. They need to be given the chance to take up work and volunteering opportunities. Parents and pundits need to stop making the world all about the children and start building in the expectation that their tastes, inclinations and demands are not the only factors that need to be taken into consideration. Recognising

13 It could be horrible, too; this is not a look back at Eden. However, it was practically unheard of for childhood gangs to involve drugs, shootings or knifings.

14 See Sian Griffiths, Children 'need to volunteer and work', *Sunday Times* (16 September 2018).

15 See Bridge, *The Significance Delusion*, ch. 14.

the existence of multiple demands in life will also encourage young people to engage the bits of the brain that 'do' context, the bigger picture, he, she, it and all the other things which will help those brains to develop more healthily.

Here are a few suggestions.

Tastes

Perhaps the biggest smacked bottom here has to be given to advertisers. However, parents must also be held to account for not delaying the gratification of their own tastes, both in terms of failing to be good role models in their own eating habits and giving in to the sweetness of letting children have what they want. Holding out against children's demands can leave a sour taste in the mouth at first but, like lemons, it's a taste that grows on us and is good for us.

Giving children a taste for fresh food, including fruit and vegetables, is not only much better for their physical health but it also helps them to understand how and where food comes from and the part that long-term planning plays in life. Not to mention that delaying gratification is critical to growing food – nothing is instant – so children will develop an understanding of the importance of both context and patience. Poor diet is also linked to obesity, which in turn is linked to depression, not simply because children can't take exercise as easily or that they are ashamed of their bodies (both good reasons to be depressed), but because of the complex interaction of the gut and the brain. Better nutrition is closely associated with better mental function, so no amount of positioning around body positivity or individual Rights should make it okay to abuse children's long-term physical and mental health.

A recent study has showed that repeated episodes of depression in people's twenties, thirties and forties are associated with a decline in mental functioning in general and with loss of memory in their fifties and the potential for dementia in older age.[16] All rather disturbing, and hopefully a reason for genuinely caring people to overrule children's demands for the food they like – 'because it's so much easier' – and to encourage them to become more taste-full eaters.

---

16 University of Sussex, Depression in your twenties linked to memory loss in your fifties, find Sussex psychologists (8 May 2019) [press release]. Available at: http://www.sussex.ac.uk/broadcast/read/48169.

Exposure

Exposure to challenging environments is a good thing. Bugs and dirt and animal life in general bring protection in ways that the manufacturers of antibacterial sprays don't want us to know about. The benefits in terms of allergies and asthma have been recognised for a while, but new research also shows that stress responses vary between urban children and those who grow up on farms.[17] City children have heightened inflammatory responses to stressful situations (courtesy of less effective immune systems). Surprisingly, they reported feeling less anxious than their rural peers when subjected to stressors, suggesting that they don't know they are stressed and therefore are unlikely to take action against it.[18] Previous research has shown that exaggerated inflammatory responses are linked to depression and the possibility of PTSD in later life.

This may not be the most obvious of associations, but it's an interesting one. It's not just that dirt can be fun, it can also keep us sane. The principle is that we should stop trying to insulate children from life and start trying to build in activities that connect them to challenges of every sort, even challenges to their physiological systems.

Inclinations

Some young people are inclined to sleep in late (but only some – not all young people fall into this category), but this doesn't mean that they should. There have been various studies which suggest that because young people's brains are developing and they have different patterns of activity from adult brains, leading to changes in the body clock and differently timed arousal levels, they would be better off with later starts in the morning and special timetabled arrangements at school.

Even if these brain differences do exist, the fact remains that people of similar ages who work in paid employment cannot ask for the

---

17 Till S. Böbel, Sascha B. Hackl, Dominik Langgartner, Marc N. Jarczok, Nicolas Rohleder, Graham A. Rook, Christopher A. Lowry, Harald Gündel, Christiane Waller and Stefan O. Reber, Less immune activation following social stress in rural vs. urban participants raised with regular or no animal contact, respectively, *Proceedings of the National Academy of Sciences of the United States of America* 115(20) (2018): 5259–5264.

18 Such as controlling it with prefrontal activity – breathing, relaxation and so on.

same allowances to be made. They just have to get on with it. Historically, adolescents took on paper rounds before attending morning classes – did they all fail dismally at school? Did the intellect and creativity of Shakespeare and every schoolboy of his generation, with 'shining morning face, creeping like a snail unwillingly to school',[19] suffer, too? And what about parents' work obligations? Where in any of this is the wider context or the appreciation of society's complex needs? It's all about the teens.

There have been suggestions that it is the blue light of digital screens that causes so much disruption to the brain behaviour of adolescents – that and the addictive lure of social media and online gaming which keeps them going late into the night and prevents them from getting the amount of sleep they need for their brains to work effectively. An extra hour of sleep per night can result in significantly better memory and problem-solving, so the most important thing that needs to be changed for teens is the total amount of sleep. The advice for young people to sleep without TVs, tablets or phones in their room and to have screen downtime for an hour before bed is reasonably well known, so it's for parents to suck the lemon and enforce the guidelines.

What may be less well known is the association between early rising and better mental health; even further reason to question the advice to let adolescents sleep in. It seems that not only are night owls at greater risk of depression, but they are also at greater risk of developing schizophrenia.[20] That is serious stuff. As teens are at the point of brain development when schizophrenia is most likely to occur, I would like to see some conclusive evidence that getting up later – later than natural light cycles would suggest – is of genuine benefit. Otherwise, I would suspect that any differences in adolescent brain behaviour have been inflated by lifestyle factors, not all of which should be encouraged.

James Tilley, professor of politics at Oxford University, raises another interesting possibility. He argues that adolescent brains are less mature than they used to be because much less maturity is now expected of them.[21] Young people are less likely to be in full-time

---

19 *As You Like It*, II, vii.

20 Rhys Blakely, Morning people have lower depression risk, *The Times* (30 January 2019).

21 James Tilley, Should the UK be raising rather than lowering the voting age?, *BBC News* (7 January 2019). Available at: https://www.bbc.co.uk/news/uk-politics-46737013.

work than in the past, and less likely to have taken on what are known as 'adult responsibilities' (see page 121) and so are growing up more slowly. He quotes an American neuroscientist, Professor Abigail Baird, who suggests that, deprived of certain adult rites of passage, the brains of young adults (by implication in Western cultures; Third World experiences will be very different) will be maturing more slowly than in the past: 'it seems very likely that if important experiences come later in life then so does brain development'. She goes on to suggest that an 18-year-old in the past would have had a brain that looked more like a 23-year-old's today.

It is an article which, slightly tongue-in-cheek, is arguing for later political power sharing; but if the evidence is correct, it may also, rather less tongue-in-cheek, be persuasive in stopping more schools from adopting policies that encourage young people to believe (a) that the world should be made to conform to them, and (b) that they are less mature than they could be and it's okay to stay that way. Let's hope the evidence which suggests that late starts and mental health problems go hand in hand will also be taken into consideration.

I hope these thoughts will kick-start some other ideas about how we might encourage young people to feel that life could be healthier and more rewarding if they saw it as being about more than just them, what they want and, of course, how they feel.

Sneaking feelings

At the start of this chapter I suggested that if I wanted to get to the point of better mental health I wouldn't be starting with feelings, I would be starting with people who have better mental health. We've now taken a look at some of them and their attributes, so it's time to get back to feelings – a theme which has dominated so much of the debate about mental health.

It has become a mantra that talking about feelings will be the solution to our current problems with mental health. Previous generations were bad at it and that was bad for them, so the thinking goes that we must all be more emotionally articulate if we want to understand ourselves better and cope more appropriately with life's challenges. But I doubt that those elderly Italians were adept at talking about feelings; talking socially about many varied matters, perhaps, but feelings? Feelings didn't crop up that much in the research findings.

However, mostly anecdotally, it does seem to be true that talking about feelings can help some people, but certainly not all. And even then, the talking has to be of a particular kind, which isn't necessarily obvious to many advocates of talking therapies. Forcing people to talk because they are 'in denial' or unable to access 'appropriate emotions' without help, is nothing short of bullying, but unfortunately that kind of bullying does happen in some therapeutic settings, self-help groups and in rehab (not all of which have professionally qualified practitioners).

Other problems with the talking approach include:

- People on the autistic spectrum (and this may be unrecognised) process language differently and have different patterns of brain connectivity, which can mean there are fewer connections between the emotion centres – the 'making sense of' areas and the language areas – so for them talking about emotions may simply mean coming up with the right script to satisfy the situation. It may also mean frustration if people demand more, and anger or fear at any demand at all.

- Talking about raw feelings can be too immersive for many people. In the case of PTSD, it can risk the client re-experiencing their trauma to such an extent that their PTSD is reinforced. Not helpful.

- Non-agentic talking, as in positioning yourself as a victim or on the receiving end of life, has been shown to produce little beneficial therapeutic effect. Only when a client can take ownership of their life and what they can affect in it, is there evidence that talking is genuinely helpful. The use of the first person pronoun 'I' is important here. Overuse of 'I', without agency, is associated with poorer mental health and even with suicidal thoughts,[22] which runs counter to the idea of talking as a cure-all.

- Ironically, too much agency can also be unhelpful. People who blame themselves for everything or who make everything about them (even if it's bad) are less likely to be exercising agency than fixating on themselves.

---

22 See again the work of James Pennebaker: Your use of pronouns reveals your personality.

● Rehearsing, repeating, revising – these are all excellent ways to implant learning, and so if a memory is either wrong (remember Elizabeth Loftus) or negatively slanted, courtesy of depression, PTSD or other mental health issues, then going over and over it without guidance (as happens in many group situations) may lead to enhanced learning of the problem thinking and problem material. They can become entrenched and 'true', with recovered memory syndrome and learned helplessness being just two of the possible outcomes.

● If substances like drugs or alcohol are being used then talking may be completely irrelevant anyway. At best they will impact heavily on the process, and it will be very hard to disentangle what gets said from the words of the beast in the brain. Alcohol may loosen the tongue, *in vino veritas* and the rest, but it's also a depressant and will bring a big lairy doom monster to the table, rather than an honest emotion broker. Most other drugs distort perception and memory to such an extent that they make for even more unreliable witnesses. Individuals need to be clean and sober before talking can be of any real benefit, which is something that university counselling services need to take into account much more. If students are using, then that should be the first matter to be addressed. Currently it is often seen as a side issue or default condition that is the outcome of a problem; it isn't often regarded as being the cause of the problem. Unlike in prisons. Funny that – could it be a form of prejudice?

● As the beautiful and famous Mitford sisters' Nanny used to say when they moaned about their clothes (even Diana's wedding dress!), 'It's all right, darling, no one's going to look at you,'[23] with the debunking emphasis on the word 'you'. If talking is going to be helpful for mental health, then as well as encouraging the talker to put their experiences, emotions, behaviours, wants and desires into a bigger and wider context (i.e. meaning making), it must also help the individual to see themselves as a part of a whole. To see that it's not all about them (although, of course, it simultaneously is); it's about them *and* their part in the whole, as both contributor and receiver, subject and object.

Resilience is less to do with endlessly delving deep into personal feelings, and more to do with feeling positive about living, about the

---

23 *Sunday Times*, Fatal attractions: the youngest Mitford sister tells her story (5 September 2010).

world and about making a significant contribution to wider society. It also helps if you can see yourself more objectively – from the outside in rather than from the inside out. Helping young people to perceive themselves as more contextualised and socially connected beings is the best pro resilience gift an adult can give.

Parenting for resilience

* Sleep – ahhh. But not all babies and small children see it that way. Matthew Walker, director of the Center for Human Sleep Science at the University of California, sees lack of sleep as one of the greatest health crises of the day: 'No aspect of our biology is left unscathed by sleep deprivation … It sinks down into every possible nook and cranny. And yet no one is doing anything about it. Things have to change: in the workplace and our communities, our homes and families.'[24] More positively, it has been shown that toddlers who take regular naps learn words faster and better, but that children who are relatively sleep poor end up vocabulary poor as well, and more at risk of obesity and behavioural disorders.[25] It really is up to parents to bear up and enforce bedtimes (as well as remove screens from bedrooms) because children haven't read the science themselves.[26]

* Children appreciate parental boundaries more than is probably obvious. Sometimes, quite often in fact, a child needs the reassurance of knowing there are such things as simple right and wrong. Not only does it make the world a more secure place, but it also takes away the responsibility of having to understand everything in the adult world, allowing a child to be a child while they can.[27] On top of the security that comes from

24 Rachel Cooke, 'Sleep should be prescribed': what those late nights out could be costing you, *The Observer* (24 September 2017).

25 Jessica Horst, Kelly Parsons and Natasha Bryan, Get the story straight: contextual repetition promotes word learning from storybooks, *Frontiers in Developmental Psychology* 2(17) (2011): 1–11.

26 See Bridge, *The Significance Delusion*, p. 237 for comments by child psychologist Tanya Byron on the risks to children's mental and physical health caused by poor parental discipline over sleep routines.

27 Read Nina Massey's article to see why even very small children appear to appreciate the value of leadership: Parents who believe in showing children who is boss 'may be on right track', *MSN News* (29 July 2019). Available at: https://www.msn.com/en-gb/news/uknews/parents-who-believe-in-showing-children-who-is-boss-%E2%80%98may-be-on-right-track%E2%80%99/ar-AAF1Q3E.

believing parents may actually have some of the answers, there is also the certainty that comes with routine for those children who understand that bedtime means bedtime. Even elderly Italians understand that routine is good for mental health, providing there is the flexibility for any necessary adaptations.

● Other principles that worked for elderly Italians – positivity, a strong work ethic and close family bonds – can all be modelled by parents. It's easy to slip into a negative relationship with children who are being tricky, but a positive attitude can be infectious. It can also undermine a child's unconscious attempts to topple parental resistance by means of emotional blackmail. Fathers can be more muscular about this kind of thing, often being less sensitive to 'atmospheres', and bringing learning advantages all of their own. British researchers found that fathers' involvement in child-rearing brought typically male advantages, such as being more vigorous and stimulating, more risk-taking and exploratory in style.[28] All of which, even when experiences are apparently negative (such as risk-taking which results in minor injuries), creates positive stress that results in better cognitive development and much greater resilience.

● Parents talking to their children is great for building family bonds – nothing focused or directed, just talking (listening implied), possibly at meal times, because eating together around a table is associated with greater interest and involvement by parents (*no* electronic gadgetry allowed – children feel their parents are in denial about mobile phone use), but also outside when walking or carrying out jobs and activities together. Family discussions are hugely significant and effective in supporting children's feelings of autonomy and responsibility. They help children to realise that they can be answerable to others for their thinking; to take ownership of their ideas, while also being prepared to revise them (a little – maybe a very little in the case of teenagers); and, very importantly, to be considered as equal stakeholders – if not equal authorities – in family matters. If parents want children to be resilient, then taking them seriously and building them up as rational people, as opposed to coming down to them in the form of being 'besties', works best. They need to know that parents have

---

28 Katherine Sellgren, Babies with involved fathers learn faster, study finds, *BBC News* (10 May 2017). Available at: https://www.bbc.co.uk/news/education-39869512. That robustness can also balance some of the sweet sentimentality of much marketing to, and parenting of, girls in particular.

(reasonable) faith in them; it helps them to feel validated and valued.

● Parents need to model desirable attitudes and behaviours.[29] Do you want your child to delay gratification, plan routines, think of others, act responsibly and be physically active? Then don't park on double yellow lines outside the school when you go to collect them at the last minute. The same applies to parking at a bus stop, in a disabled bay, across a driveway or anywhere else that is not a reasonable walk away from school. Do you want your child to avoid smoking, drinking and using other dubious substances? Then don't smoke, drink to excess or use other substances yourself – anywhere, because they will twig. The same goes for most behaviours. Do you want your child to be the best they can? Then be the best you can be – that's love.

Educating for resilience

● Poor literacy results in fewer brain connections and therefore worse overall brain health. Intensive reading remediation helps the brain to rewire and create new white matter, and more white matter equals better and healthier thought processes.[30] Helping children learn to read as fluently as possible shouldn't just be for Ofsted.

● The thinking of the moment is that children can deal with difficult topics as long as you explain all the issues to them. It's their future, so they have a right to know – about matters like climate change, the horrors of our history and why we must not be allowed to repeat the mistakes of the past. Yes, children can deal with a lot, and I have suggested they should be stakeholders in their own lives, but there is a sweet spot, and it's not in the badlands of misery. While listening to a 9-year-old's poetry written in response to a visit to a war museum, I thought

---

29 This should start before it's obvious that the child is even aware. Young children are attuned to their parents anyway, so adults who spend time on their devices in the presence of babies and toddlers make it clear to them where their priorities lie. I saw a young mum talking so distractedly on her phone that she was completely ignoring her little boy's frenzied excitement at a large piece of machinery trundling down the road. He was pointing and pointing, she was chatting and chatting. Will she expect him to tell her what he is up to when he is older?

30 Timothy Keller and Marcel Just, Altering cortical connectivity: remediation-induced changes in the white matter of poor readers, *Neuron* 64(5) (2009): 624–631.

I was hearing the words of a very old, world-weary and damaged cynic. Young children can be damaged by a diet of negativity and self-flagellation. Let's remember that the attributes of the healthily aged Italians included commitment, a sense of belonging and an optimistic outlook – none of which appeared to have been subdued by the Second World War or its effect on their country. It's not bad experiences per se that plunge people into states of permanent misery, but the drip-feeding of hopelessness and guilt.

Children have a deep-seated need for both a stable base and a reason to explore beyond it. Put simply, they need to have faith that the world is more secure than insecure, and that going out into it is more exciting than dangerous. Some adults – feeding themselves on a diet of sweet self-righteousness – seem to believe that by frightening children into tidying up the messes of the past they will somehow safeguard the future. That ain't gonna happen. Frightened children often end up angry, depressed or indifferent, which may well lead to divisions and antagonism between the generations. And that's no good for the mental health of anyone. It is much better to focus on developing attributes like curiosity and open-mindedness (both of which are mentally healthful), and helping children to find the positives in experiences which aren't of their choosing. This is quite the opposite of the fearful closing down involved in trigger warnings and safe spaces. Positivity (which is not identical to optimism or happiness) works with 'what is' rather than 'what we want to be the case' and is a foundation of resilience.

● Curiosity about the connections between information and ideas is also beneficial; mental exploration uses the same brain systems as physical exploration. Too often education is about amassing data without cross-referencing it. Although they have access to more information than ever, young people can seem strangely incurious about the world, unable to direct anyone anywhere without using their phones and blind to the ways in which science and history, for example, relate to one another. Mental capital is good for the brain; *using* mental capital to explore and make meaning is brilliant for the brain.

● Developing overview, context and perspective (all valuable in themselves) helps the rational part of the brain (our prefrontal friend) to keep tabs on what the more emotional (amygdala-biased) part of the brain is up to, which is an argument for a less topic-driven and more chronological and philosophical approach to subjects such as history. Topics can seem like islands in a sea of incomprehension for some children, especially those whose home life doesn't involve trips to places of interest.

● Gilbert Furian, who was imprisoned by the Stasi, kept himself going by seeing himself as a character in a story,[31] making meaning by using context and overview (*I was simply a bit part player, a pawn in a grand, surreal melodrama*) and externalising with second- and third-person language (*you don't have to make sense of things for yourself; he didn't feel any need to understand what was going on – it was beyond anyone's comprehension*).

● 'Owning' our stories is the mantra of the moment, alongside exploring our feelings and experiences, but education should be encouraging a wide range of genres, registers and tones, together with unpicking writers' hidden or unconscious agendas. Language, as we have seen, is a complicated tool, and young people need to learn how to understand and use it more effectively and consciously – as Furian did, to keep himself sane in a crisis.

As I observed at the beginning of this chapter, resilience – or the ability to bounce back from challenge or a crisis – is multifaceted. It may look like positivity or sociability, curiosity or work ethic, but beneath its outward face it is a brain behaviour. Inevitably, it features a lot of activity in our old chum the prefrontal area and a certain amount of damping down of activity in the amygdala, but in this chapter I have tried to explore how this works in a number of practical behavioural ways, ones which particularly apply in parenting and education. But there are a few more general tips which apply to anyone and everyone who wants to work on building their resilience, so I'm going to add these in a call to action before moving on to the grand finale.

---

31 Andrews, 'I put myself in standby mode': what makes a survivor?

Chapter 11

A call to action

Exercise

I can't say this often enough, so here goes again. It's probably no coincidence that many great writers were also great walkers. Shakespeare may or may not have chosen to be, but he probably had to cover considerable distances on foot; Jane Austen was a 'desperate walker' (i.e. enthusiastic and fast) by her own admission; and Charles Dickens was given to little night strolls from London to the Kent coast, just to collect his thoughts. The fact is that energetic movement – fast walking or running – helps us to collect (and connect) our thoughts. Runners' brains show much more functional connectivity in brain scans than the brains of more sedentary folk.[1]

Functional connectivity is associated with the linking of areas such as the hippocampus (navigation and memory) with parts which help with planning, decision-making and overall self-control. A virtuous circle is set up, making it even more likely that we can look after ourselves well in terms of both brain and body. Firmer, fitter bodies are associated with firmer, fitter brains.[2] It's a two-way street that will benefit children (children educated in or around parkland, who have to self-orientate to find their way about, have better spatial working memory which leads to greater academic achievement[3]),

1   David Raichlen, Pradyumna Bharadwaj, Megan Fitzhugh, Kari Haws, Gabrielle-Ann Torre, Theodore Trouard and Gene Alexander, Differences in resting state functional connectivity between young adult endurance athletes and healthy controls, *Frontiers in Human Neuroscience* 10(610) (2016). DOI: 10.3389/fnhum.2016.00610.

2   Fathers who run may pass on cleverer brains: runners' sperm appears to contain microRNAs which help to create better connections between brain cells in babies. See Hillary Schwarb, Curtis Johnson, Ana Daugherty, Charles Hillman, Arthur Kramer, Neal Cohen and Aron Barbey, Aerobic fitness, hippocampal viscoelasticity, and relational memory performance, *Neuroimage* 153 (2017): 179–188.

3   Note to maturing males: fast physical navigation of space, such as orienteering, has been found to be particularly protective against dementia in men. See Martin Lövdén, Sabine Schaefer, Hannes Noack, Nils Christian Bodammer, Simone Kühn, Hans-Jochen Heinze, Emrah Düzel, Lars Bäckman and Ulman Lindenberger, Spatial navigation training protects the hippocampus against age-related changes during early and late adulthood, *Neurobiology of Aging* 33(2) (2012): 620.e9–620.e22.

teenagers (they will almost certainly sleep better, too) and adults (who benefit not only in the short term but in the very long term too – ending their days with fewer age-related problems than their – let's be honest – lazier peers).

Although exercise is about as good a therapy as you can get for most things, there is exercise and exercise, and then there is over-exercise. Over-exercising is a genuine problem, especially for people with so-called 'addictive personalities'. For them, just about anything, including normally beneficial activities, can present opportunities for excess. In combination with extreme forms of dieting or food selection, over-exercisers can cause real harm to their joint and heart health. It's all about balance; for most people, the sweet spot is reasonably intensive exercise three times a week, with rest days in-between.

The type of exercise makes a difference, too; there are a lot of body-builders in prisons. Gym sessions are generally seen as a Good Thing, but there can still be problems – such as the worryingly high number of young boys trying to create perfect Instagram bodies at an age when their skeletons can't take the pressure. There is also a strong association between bodybuilding and steroid use,[4] which not only causes harm to hearts and fertility (ironically, sperm counts can become almost non-existent in Big Men), but potentially also leading to what is called 'roid rage' – a loss of anger control that sees our hot-hatch friend, the amygdala, become a red mist, rage-filled animal. Total mental wipeout is hardly in the long-term interests of good mental health. Once again, it's all about finding that sweet spot.

Aerobic exercise, if carried out with an eye on quantity and technique, seems to have few drawbacks and a great number of benefits for mental wellbeing, from oxygen flow to the brain to the promotion of neuronal connections. If it takes place in the great outdoors (rather than on a treadmill), not only does this up oxygen intake and quality, but it also brings an extra navigational element – and as we've seen, navigation is associated with better memory. The faster the navigation, the better the memory functions. Win-win big time.

---

4   James Gallagher, Fertility paradox in male beauty quest, *BBC News* (28 May 2019). Available at: https://www.bbc.co.uk/news/health-48396071.

Another form of exercise that is good for brains, and has only fairly recently been lifted out of the 'just for cranks' category, is cold-water swimming.[5] It has been claimed by many disciples as a cure-all for depression and anxiety, although there is as yet little evidence for it. However, such relatively harmless stress is probably good in itself for waking up the overall system.

Exercise comes in real-life forms as well: both gardening and housework make for excellent workouts. (Why does any halfway sane person pay for a gym membership *and* buy a leaf blower? That's plain daft.)

Diet

If we want children to take on the stakeholder status that gives them a sense of significance, identity and purpose, we should involve them in one of the most (if not *the* most) fundamental requirements and social rituals of life: food production, preparation and consumption. However, we seem to have turned these processes into the most industrial, commercial, antisocial and individualistic ones imaginable.

We have handed cooking over to online retailers of food fantasies, although the meals they market are often prepared in large commercial kitchens in industrial parks. We eat alone or together, but often isolated by technology. We eat exactly what we chose, when we choose – in a car (adverts for Deliveroo suggest having a meal delivered to your car as you drive along!), on a bus, on a train or even walking down the street.[6] We eat food grown here, there and everywhere (and anywhere); the food miles are irrelevant, even though we *so* want to save the planet. None of this is either good for our health or for our joined-up thinking.

For both we would be better off with:

- Fresh foods (as local and seasonal as possible) freshly prepared. The preparation process helps to create a sense of personal agency and can be calming – but not if done under pressure.

---

5   Chris van Tulleken, Can cold water swimming treat depression?, *BBC News* (13 September 2018). Available at: https://www.bbc.co.uk/news/health-45487187.

6   Walking and eating is associated with disruption of digestion and with an 'addiction' to instant gratification of various sorts. Digestion and gut health are now being seen as hugely important to mental health – the gut microbiome having a very close relationship with the brain. We should be taking better care of our digestion.

- As few additives and colourants as possible – their impact is uncertain but probably not beneficial.

- As little sugar as possible. Sugar is bad on bodies and minds. It is a stimulant, which affects the reward centres of the brain in similar ways to drugs, and consequently affects self-control in a full-on addictive process. First the rush, then the drop, then the desire for more. Too much sugar has also been associated with loss of cognitive capacity,[7] so the advice on sugar is pretty obvious.

- Fibre is now recognised as important for the gut, and the gut microbiome is important for brain health – so, more fibre!

- Fish and fish oils do seem to bring brain benefits, as Bertie Wooster believed, but the jury is out on the benefits of fish in cases of ADHD and similar brain problems. There is little harm, and plenty of good, in eating at least two portions of oily fish a week.

- Tryptophans are essential amino acids which are not produced by the body but are necessary to it. Low levels are associated with depression, so we should eat enough tryptophan-rich foods to boost mood. The science is a bit complicated, and the connection with depression is a little complex too, but it shouldn't be too difficult to eat more of foods like yogurt, milk, cottage cheese, bananas and turkey.

Encouraging children to tend their own veggie patch will bring rewards of just about every kind. Every school should have one and every household with a garden should have one, too.

Substances

However most of us feel about screwing around with our own physical and mental wellbeing, we generally don't feel so complacent about abusing the brains and bodies of children who have yet to be born. But how many of us know that nicotine and cannabis both damage sperm quality (and other drugs may do so, too)? I'm not going to say too much about individual substances, apart from reminding you that: (a) nicotine is a powerful gateway drug for cocaine, especially so for teenagers; (b) alcohol is a gateway drug for

---

7   Jill Barnes and Michael Joyner, Sugar highs and lows: the impact of diet on cognitive function, *Journal of Physiology* 590(12) (2012): 2831.

most undesirable substances and behaviours – quantity is all; and (c) cannabis *can* be addictive and is far more harmful than most people realise. It is also associated with psychosis and other mental health problems; the younger the age it is used, the more potentially harmful and permanent its effect. Is that enough to be going on with?

Basically, substance use boosts the hot-hatch driver at the expense of the cool classical one, which may be why substance use so often leads to doublethink and hypocrisy. I came across an example of this recently when involved in a Quit Smoking event in very green Brighton. Locals were asked for their views on banning smoking on the beach – a quandary for a city that takes its commitment to both liberty and the environment so seriously. However, it appeared that 'doing your own thing' took precedence and the majority of people declared in favour of the freedom to smoke. Cigarette butts, which are toxic and take years to biodegrade, will litter Brighton's beaches over the summer, and if washed out to sea will form part of the great tide of plastic that is destroying marine life. Where is the logic? Presumably lost to the local roll-ups – after all, they don't often have filters!

Lack of coherency and a neglect of spaces beyond the self are what you get with substance use (Brighton is a sad example of both). First, though, there is a loss of awareness of the impact of what you are doing, both on yourself and on society. Your logic seems impeccable, even as you damage the place in the brain where logic should be happening.

External observations, aka criticism

Criticism is not usually very well tolerated, even by uber-tolerant people, but as the previous section shows, we can sometimes lose perspective on our own behaviour. Individualism dictates that we get personally offended and defensive if we (or, in particular, our parenting) are ever criticised. We can enjoy these sugary feelings of hurt or offence, or we can listen, take any constructive observations on-board and maybe hit a sweeter spot where wellbeing takes precedence.

Grand finale

Fitter, healthier brains (and less emotional flab)

I have expressed a number of anti-establishment ideas in this book and made a lot of potentially controversial claims, but I have done so because I am passionate about challenging the current orthodoxy around mental health. After all, how successful are the solutions that are currently being offered up? Problems seem to be getting worse by the minute,[1] but despite that the unsubstantiated and often self-interested rhetoric goes on.

I expect some kick back, but hold that counter-knee-jerk-reaction just for a moment. Rather than assuming that what is being promoted *should* work, ask yourself, 'Does it work?' 'Is it working?' 'Where is the evidence that what we've been trying to do over the past few years has had any beneficial effect?' But do not ask yourself, 'Does it *feel* right?'

And then, think about what I've written again. It's not all about you and how you want to feel about yourself – or is it? Because wouldn't that mean feeding yourself on sweet sentimentality, rather than on the roughage of rational thinking (and by now we should all be on message about the bodily advantages of fibre over sugar)?

Here is an even tougher question: could we be talking ourselves into an even worse place than the one we're already in? If constant exposure to ideas and images of self-harm on the internet is to be blamed for the rise in cases of self-harm, why shouldn't the same thinking

---

1   Oliver Newlan, Antidepressant prescriptions for children on the rise, *BBC News* (28 July 2018). Available at: https://www.bbc.co.uk/news/health-44821886; Sian Griffiths and Tim Shipman, 'Suicidal generation': tragic toll of teenagers double in eight years, *Sunday Times* (3 February 2019).

apply to mental health problems?[2] There are days when mental distress seems to be the only issue on the news agenda, but is this genuinely helpful or mostly a case of media/celebrity virtue signalling?

Maybe it is simply another example of the single issue silo thinking that might itself be the outcome of a lack of bigger picture thinking. We see a pattern in one form of behaviour (exposure to self-harm content → more cases of self-harm), but we don't question whether that pattern might carry over to another example of behaviour (exposure to mental distress content → more cases of mental distress). We're just not cross-referencing.

Seeing the bigger picture, looking at the before and after, considering the wider perspective, the *alternative* perspective, thinking the problem through – all these phrases aren't simply dull old farts' advice, they are brain behaviours associated with better mental health. And knowing that bit more about the brain and how it works can help us all to worry a bit less about the sheer impossibility of the challenges we face with mental health, and to do a bit more practically – rather than noisily, emotionally and self-gratifyingly – to help.

By calling mental health 'brain health' we can also defuse some of the explosive panic about what is going on at the moment and replace it with a greater level of pragmatism. And that means doing more of what works and less of what feels good – which is, of course, associated with our old friend the cool classical one (as panic is with our other old acquaintance, the hot-hatch amygdala). Or to put it another way, we can shut off the sugar supply that has been driving our Big Feelings around mental health (which risks creating a generation of emotionally obese youngsters as we encourage them in a taste for similarly sweet emotions) and instead boost our gutsy resilience. (See what I did there?)

Now for a final round-up of words and phrases which are central to what I've been conjuring up in this book. With a nod to Sherlock, and remembering the importance of a well-functioning hippocampus to memory and mental health, it is time to create your own mind palace to store them up for future use.

---

2   Similarly, the relentless focus on harmful behaviours as part of the government's flagship Sex Offender Treatment Programme (SOTP) increased the unhealthy thought processes of convicted sex offenders. The scheme was scrapped in 2017 after research showed that participants were at a higher risk of reoffending. See Danny Shaw, Sex offender: 'I've never had so many deviant thoughts', *BBC News* (8 October 2019). Available at: https://www.bbc.co.uk/news/uk-49973318.

Amygdala, aka **hot-hatch** driver, aka emotional nuclear fuel bunker, aka red mist/rage primitive. Like King Lear, this part of the brain, though often voluble, tends to be incoherent when it comes to making sense of itself: 'I will do such things – What they are yet I know not, but they shall be the terrors of the earth.'[3]

The **bigger picture** widens our perspective and takes on board the needs and considerations of multiple factors and people, reducing self-absorption.

Connections help us to make meaning or make sense of things, whether they are between our neurons or between the things beyond our heads.

The **cool classical one**, our **prefrontal friend** keeps everything, even the hot amygdala, under control – perhaps occasionally a little too much.

Curiosity about life and the world turns our attention outwards and encourages healthy mental and physical exploration.

Delaying gratification is the ability to sit with feelings stirred up by hot stimuli until the impulses die down and better decisions can be made.

A **diet of sweet sentiment** is one which risks emotional obesity.

A **diet of fibre** is one which results in a greater ability to exercise both body and self-control.

---

3   *King Lear*, II, iv.

The **hippocampus** – the 'sea horse' in the brain – helps us to navigate and remember, and then navigate our memories, right on into old age if we're lucky.

Identity is not as fixed as we sometimes like to believe, any more than is image.

I, myself and me is a much more fixed affair – no doubt about the 'fixation' here!

Happiness can be a mixed blessing.

Memory can be a mixed blessing, too, but only if it keeps going round in a loop (obsession or PTSD) or stops altogether (dementia); otherwise, it helps to keep us both healthy and sane.

Navigation and memory are close companions and tread the same ground – they need each other.

Perfectionism, though, is just fine as it is! No room for nuance or middle ground allowed.

Resilience is, quite simply, at the heart of everything.

The **selfie**. The self is at the heart, and in the focus, of everything.

The **sweet spot** is where balance lies – somewhere that is truly the best for mental health.

We can achieve a better balance by connecting, connecting, connecting – brain and body, thoughts and voice, sentiment and sense, I and we, me and us, you and them, past and present, now and future, here and there, good and bad, love and hate, old and young, man and woman, friend and foe, and always, always, always – hot hatch and cool classical.

And that is the story of how we, as individuals, can be good for our brains. If enough of us spread the story around as we go about our daily business, creating that viral meme I alluded to in the introduction, we will have a much bigger impact on the mental health crisis than any amount of sweet sentiment or hot-hatch anger by pressure groups, activists, celebs and politicos could ever do.

References

Al-Mosaiwi, Mohammed (2018) People with depression use language differently – here's how to spot it, *The Conversation* (2 February). Available at: http://theconversation.com/people-with-depression-use-language-differently-heres-how-to-spot-it-90877.

Al-Mosaiwi, Mohammed and Tom Johnstone (2018) In an absolute state: elevated use of absolutist words is a marker specific to anxiety, depression, and suicidal ideation, *Clinical Psychological Science* 6(4): 529–542. Available at: https://journals.sagepub.com/doi/full/10.1177/2167702617747074.

Andrews, Tony (2017) 'I put myself in standby mode': what makes a survivor?, *The Guardian* (7 January). Available at: https://www.theguardian.com/society/2017/jan/07/put-myself-standby-mode-what-makes-a-survivor.

Bannerman, Lucy and Tatiana Hepher (2019) You can't have it all, admits Cosmopolitan editor Farrah Storr, *The Times* (29 September).

Barford, Duncan (2018) Dark night of the soul, *Therapy Today* 29(6): 34–37.

Barnes, Jill and Michael Joyner (2012) Sugar highs and lows: the impact of diet on cognitive function, *Journal of Physiology* 590(12): 2831.

Barrie, Douglas (2019) Veterans who serve longer live on, *The Scotsman* (20 March).

BBC News (2018) Cannabis 'more harmful than alcohol' for teen brains (3 October). Available at: https://www.bbc.co.uk/news/health-45732911.

BBC News (2018) Fall in strength and fitness of 10-year-olds, study shows (26 September). Available at: https://www.bbc.co.uk/news/health-45651719.

Bedrosian, Tracy A., Carolina Quayle, Nicole Novaresi and Fred. H. Gage (2018) Early life experience drives structural variation of neural genomes in mice, *Science* 359(6382): 1395–1399.

Bennett, Rosemary (2017) We've never had it so good: 1957 was the happiest year, *The Times* (24 January).

Berret, Emmanuelle, Michael Kintscher, Shriya Palchaudhuri, Wei Tang, Denys Osypenko, Olexiy Kochubey and Ralf Schneggenburger (2019) Insular cortex processes aversive somatosensory information and is crucial for threat learning, *Science* 364(6443): eaaw0474.

Blakely, Rhys (2019) Morning people have lower depression risk, *The Times* (30 January).

Böbel, Till S., Sascha B. Hackl, Dominik Langgartner, Marc N. Jarczok, Nicolas Rohleder, Graham A. Rook, Christopher A. Lowry, Harald Gündel, Christiane Waller and Stefan O. Reber (2018) Less immune activation following social stress in rural vs. urban participants raised with regular or no animal contact, respectively, *Proceedings of the National Academy of Sciences of the United States of America* 115(20): 5259–5264.

Bodkin, Henry (2019) Tens of thousands of UK children have PTSD due to bullying and violence, Lancet study finds, *The Telegraph* (22 February). Available at: https://www.telegraph.co.uk/news/2019/02/22/tens-thousands-uk-children-have-ptsd-due-bullying-violence-lancet.

Bowlby, John (1969) *Attachment and Loss, Vol. 1: Attachment* (New York: Basic Books).

Bridge, Gillian (2016) *The Significance Delusion: Unlocking Our Thinking for Our Children's Future* (Carmarthen: Crown House Publishing).

Calaprice, Alice (ed.) (2005) *The New Quotable Einstein* (Princeton, NJ: Princeton University Press).

Carter, Sue (2019) The biology of 'love': lessons from prairie voles, *Open Access Government* (2 April). Available at: https://www.openaccessgovernment.org/prairie-voles/62218.

Cartwright Hatton, Sam (2018) Running in the family: can we help anxious parents to raise confident children? Lecture delivered at Brighton and Sussex Medical School, University of Sussex, 11 April.

Chiu, Pearl H., Terry Lohrenz and P. Read Montague (2008) Smokers' brains compute, but ignore, a fictive error signal in a sequential investment task, *Nature Neuroscience* 11(4): 514–520.

Cohen, Deborah and Hannah Barnes (2019) Transgender treatment: puberty blockers study under investigation, *BBC News* (22 July). Available at: https://www.bbc.co.uk/news/health-49036145.

Comings, David and Kenneth Blum (2000) Reward deficiency syndrome: genetic aspects of behavioral disorders, *Progress in Brain Research* 126: 325–341.

Cooke, Rachel (2017) 'Sleep should be prescribed': what those late nights out could be costing you, *The Observer* (24 September).

Coughlan, Sean (2018) How do career dreams really work out?, *BBC News* (27 September). Available at: https://www.bbc.co.uk/news/education-45666030.

Curran, Thomas and Andrew P. Hill (2017) Perfectionism is increasing over time: a meta-analysis of birth cohort differences from 1989 to 2016, *Psychological Bulletin* 145(4): 410–429.

Day, Jonathan, Soham Savani, Benjamin Krempley, Matthew Nguyen and Joanna Kitlinska (2016) Influence of paternal preconception exposures on their offspring: through epigenetics to phenotype, *American Journal of Stem Cells* 5(1): 11–18.

Denkova, Ekaterina, Sandra Dolcos and Florin Dolcos (2015) Neural correlates of 'distracting' from emotion during autobiographical recollection, *Social Cognitive and Affective Neuroscience* 10(2): 219–230.

Drug and Alcohol Findings (2017) Hot topics. It's magic: prevent substance use problems without mentioning drugs (23 January). Available at: https://findings.org.uk/PHP/dl.php?file=hot_no_drugs.hot.

Dunbar, Jordan (2019) Cavemen therapy: can being a caveman cure anxiety?, *BBC News* (3 August) [video]. Available at: https://www.bbc.co.uk/news/av/health-49211802/cavemen-therapy-can-being-a-caveman-cure-anxiety.

Ecclestone, Kathryn (2016) The effects of a 'vulnerability zeitgeist' in universities: real need or real life?, *University and College Counselling* 4(3): 4–9.

Ehrenreich, Barbara (2018) *Natural Causes: Life, Death and the Illusion of Control* (London: Granta).

Farias, Miguel and Catherine Wikholm (2015) *The Buddha Pill: Can Meditation Change You?* (London: Watkins Publishing).

Flack, Zoe M. and Jessica S. Horst (2018) Two sides to every story: children learn words better from one storybook page at a time, *Infant and Child Development* 27(1): e2047.

Ford, Brett, Phoebe Lam, Oliver John and Iris Mauss (2018) The psychological health benefits of accepting negative emotions and thoughts: laboratory, diary, and longitudinal evidence, *Journal of Personality and Social Psychology* 115(6): 1075–1092.

Gallagher, James (2019) Fertility paradox in male beauty quest, *BBC News* (28 May). Available at: https://www.bbc.co.uk/news/health-48396071.

Geddes, Linda (2016) Self-mastery can be yours with three pillars of emotional wisdom, *New Scientist* (2 January). Available at: https://www.newscientist.com/article/mg22930540-800-self-mastery-can-be-yours-with-three-pillars-of-emotional-wisdom.

George, Alison (2018) Memory special: do we even know what memory is for?, *New Scientist* (24 October). Available at: https://www.newscientist.com/article/mg24032010-500-memory-special-do-we-even-know-what-memory-is-for.

Ghosh, Pallab (2019) AAAS: machine learning 'causing science crisis', *BBC News* (16 February). Available at: https://www.bbc.co.uk/news/science-environment-47267081.

Golding, Jean, Genette Ellis, Steven Gregory, Karen Birmingham, Yasmin Iles-Caven, Dheeraj Rai and Marcus Pembrey (2017) Grandmaternal smoking in pregnancy and grandchild's autistic traits and diagnosed autism, *Scientific Reports* 7, article 46179. DOI: 10.1038/srep46179.

Gorham, Lisa, Terry Jernigan, Jim Hudziak and Deanna Barch (2019) Involvement in sports, hippocampal volume, and depressive symptoms in children, *Biological Psychiatry: Cognitive Neuroscience and Neuroimaging* 4(5): 484–492.

Greene, Graham (2004 [1948]) *The Heart of the Matter* (London: Vintage).

Griffiths, Sian (2017a) Feckless boys blamed on 'best friend' fathers, *Sunday Times* (2 April).

Griffiths, Sian (2017b) 'Gromp' schools romp to top of class, *Sunday Times* (20 August).

Griffiths, Sian (2018) Children 'need to volunteer and work', *Sunday Times* (16 September).

Griffiths, Sian and Tim Shipman (2019) 'Suicidal generation': tragic toll of teenagers double in eight years, *Sunday Times* (3 February).

Haines, Jess, Sheryl Rifas-Shiman, Nicholas Horton, Ken Kleinman, Katherine Bauer, Kirsten Davison, Kathryn Walton, S. Bryn Austin, Alison Field and Matthew Gillman (2016) Family functioning and quality of parent–adolescent relationship: cross-sectional associations with adolescent weight-related behaviors and weight status, *International Journal of Behavioral Nutrition and Physical Activity* 13, article 68. DOI: 10.1186/s12966-016-0393-7.

Harding-Jones, Cate (2019) Counselling survivors of sex trafficking, *Therapy Today* (23 February). Available at: https://www.bacp.co.uk/bacp-journals/therapy-today/2019/february-2019.

Hellen, Nicholas (2016) Speech therapy for 3-year-olds who shove to make friends, *Sunday Times* (4 December).

Horst, Jessica, Kelly Parsons and Natasha Bryan (2011) Get the story straight: contextual repetition promotes word learning from storybooks, *Frontiers in Developmental Psychology* 2(17): 1–11.

Hughes, Claire, Rory Devine, Judi Mesman and Clancy Blair (2019) Parental wellbeing, couple relationship quality and children's behavior problems in the first two years of life, *Development & Psychopathology* 8: 597–600.

Hurst, Greg (2018) Why daddy's girls can cope better with setbacks, *The Times* (30 August).

Ives, Laurel (2019) NHS child gender reassignment 'too quick', *BBC News* (25 February). Available at: https://www.bbc.co.uk/news/health-47359692.

Jackson, Catherine (2019) Who needs a diagnosis?, *Therapy Today* (8 February). Available at: https://www.bacp.co.uk/bacp-journals/therapy-today/2019/february-2019/who-needs-a-diagnosis.

Jamison, Kay Redfield (1993) *Touched with Fire: Manic-Depressive Illness and the Artistic Temperament* (New York: Free Press).

Katsumi, Yuta and Sandra Dolcos (2018) Suppress to feel and remember less: neural correlates of explicit and implicit emotional suppression on perception and memory, *Neuropsychologia*. DOI: 10.1016/j.neuropsychologia.2018.02.010.

Keeley, Graham (2018) War hero, 100, given a fitting birthday treat, *The Times* (20 September).

Keller, Timothy and Marcel Just (2009) Altering cortical connectivity: remediation-induced changes in the white matter of poor readers, *Neuron* 64(5): 624–631.

Kim, Aekyoung and Sam Maglio (2018) Vanishing time in the pursuit of happiness, *Psychonomic Bulletin & Review* 25(4): 1337–1342.

Lay, Kat (2018) New surgeons 'lack dexterity after too much screen-time', *The Times* (31 October).

Lay, Kat (2019) Self-harm hospital admissions for children double in 6 years, *The Times* (23 February).

Lehrer, Jonah (2009) Don't! The secret of self-control, *The New Yorker* (11 May). Available at: https://www.newyorker.com/magazine/2009/05/18/dont-2.

Lockwood Estrin, Georgia, Elizabeth G. Ryan, Kylee Trevillion and Jill Demilew (2019) Young pregnant women and risk for mental disorders: findings from an early pregnancy cohort, *British Journal of Psychiatry Open* 5(2): e21. DOI: https://doi.org/10.1192/bjo.2019.6.

Lövdén, Martin, Sabine Schaefer, Hannes Noack, Nils Christian Bodammer, Simone Kühn, Hans-Jochen Heinze, Emrah Düzel, Lars Bäckman and Ulman Lindenberger (2012) Spatial navigation training protects the hippocampus against age-related changes during early and late adulthood, *Neurobiology of Aging* 33(2): 620.e9–620.e22.

Maguire, Eleanor A., David G. Gadian, Ingrid S. Johnsrude, Catriona D. Good, John Ashburner, Richard S. J. Frackowiak and Christopher D. Frith (2000) Navigation-related structural change in the hippocampi of taxi drivers, *Proceedings of the National Academy of Sciences of the United States of America* 97(8): 4398–4403.

Maier, Steven F., Jose Amat, Michael V. Baratta, Evan Paul and Linda R. Watkins (2006) Behavioural control, the medial prefrontal cortex, and resilience, *Dialogues Clinical Neuroscience* 8(4): 397–406.

Massey, Nina (2019) Parents who believe in showing children who is boss 'may be on right track', *MSN News* (29 July). Available at: https://www.msn.com/en-gb/news/uknews/parents-who-believe-in-showing-children-who-is-boss-%E2%80%98may-be-on-right-track%E2%80%99/ar-AAF1Q3E.

Moser, Jason, Adrienne Dougherty, Whitney Mattson, Benjamin Katz, Tim Moran, Darwin Guevarra, Holly Shablack, Ozlem Ayduk, John Jonides, Marc Berman and Ethan Kross (2017) Third person self-talk facilitates emotion regulation without engaging cognitive control: converging evidence from ERP and fMRI, *Scientific Reports* 7, article 4519. DOI: 10.1038/s41598-017-04047-3.

National Literacy Trust (2018) Life expectancy shortened by 26 years for children growing up in areas with the most serious literacy problems (15 February) [press release]. Available at: https://literacytrust.org.uk/news/life-expectancy-shortened-26-years-children-growing-areas-most-serious-literacy-problems.

Newlan, Oliver (2018) Antidepressant prescriptions for children on the rise, *BBC News* (28 July). Available at: https://www.bbc.co.uk/news/health-44821886.

Newsbeat (2019) London knife crime: 'I don't know how many people I've stabbed', *BBC News* (13 February 2019). Available at: https://www.bbc.co.uk/news/newsbeat-47211971.

NHS (2017) *Mental Health of Children and Young People in England*. Available at: https://digital.nhs.uk/data-and-information/publications/statistical/mental-health-of-children-and-young-people-in-england/2017/2017.

Nichols, Tom (2019) Don't let students run the university, *The Atlantic* (7 May). Available at: https://www.theatlantic.com/ideas/archive/2019/05/camille-paglia-protests-represent-dangerous-trend/588859.

Northstone, Kate, Jean Golding, George Davey Smith, Laura Miller and Marcus Pembrey (2014) Prepubertal start of father's smoking and increased body fat in his sons: further characterisation of paternal transgenerational responses, *European Journal of Human Genetics* 22(12): 1382–1386.

Nutt, Amy Ellis (2018) Robin Williams's suicide was followed by a sharp rise in 'copycat' deaths, *Washington Post* (7 February). Available at: https://www.washingtonpost.com/news/to-your-health/wp/2018/02/07/robin-williamss-suicide-was-followed-by-a-sharp-rise-in-copycat-deaths.

O'Connor, Eimear, Teresa McCormack and Aidan Feeney (2014) Do children who experience regret make better decisions? A developmental study of the behavioral consequences of regret, *Child Development* 85(5): 1995–2010.

Parker, Olivia (2016) Should happiness be part of the school curriculum?, *The Telegraph* (11 July). Available at: https://www.telegraph.co.uk/education/2016/07/11/should-happiness-be-part-of-the-school-curriculum.

Pennebaker, James W. (2011) Your use of pronouns reveals your personality, *Harvard Business Review* (December). Available at: https://hbr.org/2011/12/your-use-of-pronouns-reveals-your-personality.

Priest, Alan (2011) Let's you and I talk, *Therapy Today* 22(10): 24–28.

Raichlen, David, Pradyumna Bharadwaj, Megan Fitzhugh, Kari Haws, Gabrielle-Ann Torre, Theodore Trouard and Gene Alexander (2016) Differences in resting state functional connectivity between young adult endurance athletes and healthy controls, *Frontiers in Human Neuroscience* 10(610). DOI: 10.3389/fnhum.2016.00610.

Roberts, Michelle (2019) Potent cannabis increases risk of serious mental illness, says study, *BBC News* (20 March). Available at: https://www.bbc.co.uk/news/health-47609849.

Robson, David (2019) Finding our voice, *New Scientist* 242(3228): 34–37.

Russell, Stephen and Jessica Fish (2016) Mental health in gay, bisexual, and transgender youth, *Annual Review of Clinical Psychology* 12(1): 465–487.

Salmond, Claire, David Menon, Doris Chatfield, John Pickard and Barbara Sahakian (2005) Deficits in decision-making in head injury survivors, *Journal of Neurotrauma* 22(6): 613–622.

Scelzo, Anna, Salvatore Di Somma, Paola Antonini, Lori Montross, Nicholas Schork, David Brenner and Dilip Jeste (2018) Mixed-methods quantitative–qualitative study of 29 nonagenarians and centenarians in rural Southern Italy: focus on positive psychological traits, *International Psychogeriatrics* 30(1): 31–38.

Schleicher, Andreas (2017) Parents make a big difference just by talking, *BBC News* (19 April). Available at: www.bbc.co.uk/news/business-39577514.

Schwarb, Hillary, Curtis Johnson, Ana Daugherty, Charles Hillman, Arthur Kramer, Neal Cohen and Aron Barbey (2017) Aerobic fitness, hippocampal viscoelasticity, and relational memory performance, *Neuroimage* 153: 179–188.

Sellgren, Katherine (2017) Babies with involved fathers learn faster, study finds, *BBC News* (10 May). Available at: https://www.bbc.co.uk/news/education-39869512.

Shaw, Danny (2019) Sex offender: 'I've never had so many deviant thoughts', *BBC News* (8 October). Available at: https://www.bbc.co.uk/news/uk-49973318.

Siddique, Haroon (2018) Middle-class cocaine users are hypocrites, says Met chief, *The Guardian* (31 July). Available at: https://www.theguardian.com/society/2018/jul/31/middle-class-cocaine-users-are-hypocrites-says-met-chief-cressida-dick.

Smiles, Samuel (1859) *Self-Help; With Illustrations of Character and Conduct* (London: John Murray).

Southgate, Ed (2019) Freshers declaring mental illness up 73% in 4 years, *The Times* (22 February).

Stirman, Shannon W. and James W. Pennebaker (2001) Word use in the poetry of suicidal and nonsuicidal poets, *Psychosomatic Medicine* 63(4): 517–522.

Stubley, Peter (2019) Chemistry student dies suddenly in 13th suspected suicide at Bristol University in three years, *The Independent* (10 August). Available at: https://www.independent.co.uk/news/uk/home-news/student-death-suicide-bristol-university-maria-stancliffe-cook-a9051606.html.

Sunday Times (2010) Fatal attractions: the youngest Mitford sister tells her story (5 September).

Tamir, Maya, Shalom Schwartz, Shige Oishi and Min Kim (2017) The secret to happiness: feeling good or feeling right?, *Journal of Experimental Psychology: General* 146(10): 1448–1459. Available at: https://www.apa.org/pubs/journals/releases/xge-xge0000303.pdf.

Taylor, Gemma, Ann McNeill, Alan Girling, Amanda Farley, Nicola Lindson-Hawley and Paul Aveyard (2014) Change in mental health after smoking cessation: systematic review and meta-analysis, *BMJ* 348: g1151.

The Conversation (2016) Smoking during pregnancy may lead to later substance use in the child (6 December). Available at: http://theconversation.com/smoking-during-pregnancy-may-lead-to-later-substance-use-in-the-child-69929.

Tilley, James (2019) Should the UK be raising rather than lowering the voting age?, *BBC News* (7 January). Available at: https://www.bbc.co.uk/news/uk-politics-46737013.

Turner, Janice (2018) Trans teenagers have become an experiment, *The Times* (18 August).

University of Sussex (2019) Depression in your twenties linked to memory loss in your fifties, find Sussex psychologists (8 May) [press release]. Available at: http://www.sussex.ac.uk/broadcast/read/48169.

US Department of Health and Human Services (2004) *The Health Consequences of Smoking. A Report of the Surgeon General* (Rockville, MD: US Department of Health and Human Services, Public Health Service, Office of the Surgeon General).

Van Dillen, Lotte, Dirk Heslenfeld and Sander Koole (2009) Tuning down the emotional brain: an fMRI study of the effects of cognitive load on the processing of affective images, *Neuroimage* 45(4): 1212–1219.

van Staden, Werdie (1999) *Linguistic Changes During Recovery: A Philosophical and Empirical Study of First Person Pronoun Usage and the Semantic Positions of Patients as Expressed in Psychotherapy and Mental Illness.* Unpublished dissertation, University of Warwick.

van Staden, Werdie (2003) Linguistic markers of recovery: theoretical underpinnings of first person pronoun usage and semantic positions of patients, *Philosophy, Psychiatry and Psychology* 9(2): 105–121

van Tulleken, Chris (2018) Can cold water swimming treat depression?, *BBC News* (13 September). Available at: https://www.bbc.co.uk/news/health-45487187.

Watts, Tyler W., Greg J. Duncan and Haonan Quan (2018) Revisiting the marshmallow test: a conceptual replication investigating links between early delay of gratification and later outcomes, *Psychological Science* 29(7): 1159–1177.

Whipple, Tom (2017a) Having a few beers is the best way to maintain male friendships, *The Times* (20 February).

Whipple, Tom (2017b) Why belief in a fair world kills poor children's hopes and dreams, *The Times* (20 June).

Wilson, Cherry (2018) We have FOMOMG – do you?, *BBC News* (22 October). Available at: https://www.bbc.co.uk/news/uk-45894506.

Wilson, Clare (2018) Memory special: can you trust your memories?, *New Scientist* (27 October). Available at: https://www.newscientist.com/article/mg24032010-700-memory-special-can-you-trust-your-memories.

Woolcock, Nicola (2016) Learning by heart is better for brain, *The Times* (31 October).

Woolcock, Nicola (2019) Grammars are not key to happiness, parents told, *The Times* (1 March).

Ye, Yvaine (2018) Nicotine exposure in male mice may trigger ADHD in their offspring, *New Scientist* (16 October). Available at: https://www.newscientist.com/article/2182614-nicotine-exposure-in-male-mice-may-trigger-adhd-in-their-offspring.

Young, Laura, Ellen Winner and Sara Cordes (2013) Heightened incidence of depressive symptoms in adolescents involved in the arts, *Psychology of Aesthetics, Creativity, and the Arts* 7(2): 197–202.

Young, Sarah (2019) Teenagers expect to earn triple the average salary by the time they turn 30, *The Independent* (13 February). Available at: https://www.independent.co.uk/life-style/teenagers-salary-dream-job-work-career-survey-a8777151.html.

Lightning Source UK Ltd.
Milton Keynes UK
UKHW021255290822
407874UK00010B/224